Unraveling
False Prophets

Unraveling
False Prophets

*A Journey of Discernment and
True Faith*

DOMINGOS AIOLFE

We dedicate this book to all believers who, with sincerity of heart, seek true spirituality and discernment in the divine words. May these pages be a source of inspiration and wisdom to strengthen your faith journeys.

To those who, like wise counselors and spiritual guides, share their knowledge and insight with love and dedication, we offer our gratitude for lighting our paths in the search for truth.

To those who, at some point, felt seduced by the empty promises of false prophets, we wish them to find redemption and the renewal of their faith through sincere repentance.

We dedicate this book to the leaders of the churches established by Christ, who are beacons of hope and solid foundations for believers in their spiritual walk. May they continue to be examples of humility and commitment to the true word of God.

To those who found the light at the end of the tunnel and, through an awakening of conscience, rediscovered true communion with the Lord, we express our admiration for their perseverance and desire for spiritual growth.

Finally, we dedicate this book to God, the source of all wisdom and insight, whose mercy is infinite and whose unconditional love guides and protects us in our search for truth. May He continue to be our rock and our refuge every moment of our spiritual journey.

May dedication and commitment in the pursuit of true spirituality be rewarded with a deeper connection with the Lord and a life enriched by divine wisdom.

"Ye shall know the truth, and the truth shall make you free." - John 8:32

In this epigraph, we find the essence of the search for truth and spiritual discernment. May these words from the Gospel of John be an inspiration to all who seek true wisdom and liberation on their spiritual journey.

Preface

It is with great joy and humility that we present this book, the result of a journey of reflection, study and devotion. In the pages that follow, we seek to explore a fundamental theme for the Christian faith: the discernment between true divine teachings and the illusions of false prophets.

Throughout the chapters, we have endeavored to examine the importance of discerning the voices clamoring for our spiritual attention. Inspired by the Holy Scriptures, we delve into the stories of sincere prophets, as well as those who were lost in the crooked paths of presumption.

Through the study of biblical passages, lessons from the history of the Church and reports of believers who faced the challenge of discernment, we seek to offer a comprehensive view on the subject. Our goal is to strengthen readers' faith and enable them to discern between the voices that echo in their hearts, so that they can draw ever closer to the true will of God.

Thanks

We would like to express our gratitude to all the people and sources who have contributed to the realization of this book. Without the support, inspiration and dedication of each one, this work would not have been possible.

First, we thank God, the supreme guide and source of inspiration for all of us. His eternal words in the Holy Scriptures were the foundation on which we built each chapter of this work, and His divine wisdom enlightened us in our journey of reflection and study.

To our family and friends, our deepest thanks for your unconditional love and encouragement. You were a constant source of support and motivation, encouraging us to move forward even in the face of challenges.

To our editorial team, who worked tirelessly to improve every detail of this book, we thank you for your dedication and professionalism in transforming our words into a meaningful work.

We also want to thank the spiritual leaders and religious guides who, with their wisdom and insight, guided us on our journey of understanding faith and divine truth.

To the readers, for choosing to embark with us on this journey of reflection and spiritual growth, we thank you for the trust placed in our work. We sincerely hope that the words contained in these pages can be a source of inspiration and enrichment in your lives.

Ultimately, we want to dedicate this book to the glory of God, the service of truth, and the continual quest for spiritual insight. May these words resonate in the hearts of readers, inspiring them to walk towards the light of truth and divine wisdom.

May the Lord's grace always be with us in our search for truth, and may our hearts remain open to hear His voice and follow His teachings.

SUMMARY

THE DIVINE WARNING

For centuries, the word of God has warned us about the presence of false prophets, whose objective is to deceive and lead the faithful away from the true path of faith. These unscrupulous pastors make unfounded revelations, propagate empty prophecies, and offer unfounded hopes. In this first chapter, we will explore the importance of discerning such figures, protecting ourselves from their deceptive tricks.

1

The Holy Bible, as a source of teaching and spiritual guide for Christians, brings several warnings about false prophets and the need to be attentive to them. Let's analyze some passages that highlight the relevance of this divine warning:

Matthew 7:15-20 "Beware of false prophets, which come to you in sheep's clothing, but inwardly they are ravening wolves. By their fruit you will know them. Are grapes gathered from thornbushes or figs from thistles? So every good tree bears good fruit, and every bad tree bears bad fruit. A good tree cannot bear bad fruit, nor can a bad tree bear good fruit. Every tree that does not produce good fruit is cut down and thrown into the fire. Therefore by their fruits you will know them."

In this passage, Jesus warns us to be attentive to the fruits produced by the prophets. The true prophets bring teachings that lead to eternal life, while the false prophets, due to their corrupt nature, end up leading people to error and perdition.

Matthew 24:11 "And many false prophets shall arise, and shall deceive many."

Here, Jesus anticipates the arrival of false prophets and warns us not to be deceived by their words and actions. It is a clear exhortation for us to be prepared to face the challenges posed by these misleading figures.

2 Pedro 2:1 "So, too, false teachers will arise among you, who will secretly introduce destructive heresies, even to the point of denying the Sovereign Lord who bought them, bringing sudden destruction upon themselves."

The apostle Peter, in his letter, reinforces the possibility of false teachers and the danger they represent when spreading erroneous doctrines. He calls our attention to the fact that these individuals can be subtle in their approach, presenting themselves as servants of God, but actually undermining true faith.

1 John 4:1 "Beloved, believe not every spirit, but try the spirits whether they are of God, because many false prophets are gone out into the world."

The apostle John emphasizes the importance of discerning the spiritual source of the messages we receive. Not everything that presents itself as spiritual or divine comes from God. Therefore, it is our duty to carefully test and evaluate the teachings and prophecies we encounter, to ensure that they are in line with the true word of God.

Jeremiah 23:16 "Thus saith the Lord of hosts; Hearken not to the words of the prophets which prophesy among you: they teach you vanity, and speak out of the strength of their own heart, not out of the mouth of the Lord."

Jeremiah, an Old Testament prophet, denounces false prophets who proclaim empty messages, originating from their own hearts and not inspired by the Lord. This reminds us to be judicious in receiving messages that claim divine authority, always seeking the truth in God and His Word.

These biblical passages are just a few of the many warnings about false prophets found throughout the Scriptures. They remind us of the importance of being aware of the signs that reveal the deceitful intentions of these figures and urge us to strengthen our faith and knowledge of the Word of God to resist their wiles.

Jesus Christ himself, our Lord and Savior, warned us about the presence of false prophets, emphasizing the importance of discerning between the true and the false. He urges us to observe the fruit produced by these individuals, for their actions will reveal the true nature of their motivations and teachings.

False prophets often present themselves as sheep, but they are ravening wolves in disguise. They may use religious language and appear to be highly spiritual, but their intentions are malicious and ultimately seek only their own interests and benefits.

Discernment is a virtue that all Christians should seek to develop. Through studying the Word of God, praying and strengthening our personal relationship with the Lord, we can acquire the wisdom needed to recognize false doctrines and unmask deceivers.

It is important to remember that false prophets are not only a threat to those less educated in the faith, but also to the most devout and knowledgeable of the Scriptures. They have the ability to distort and manipulate divine truths, presenting them in a subtle and convincing way, in order to attract even the most faithful.

However, the Word of God is a light that guides us and illuminates the true path. She is the antidote to the deceitful teachings of false prophets. When we meditate on the Scriptures, we fortify ourselves against the heresies and lies that try to undermine our faith.

We must also remember that discernment is not a purely intellectual skill, but a matter of the heart. It takes humility and willingness to listen to the voice of the Holy Spirit, who guides us to the truth. We must seek an intimate relationship with God and allow His Word to transform our minds and hearts so that we are not easily influenced by the deceptions of false prophets.

In addition to individual discernment, the Christian community also plays a key role in protecting against false prophets. Together, as members of the body of Christ, we can encourage and help each other to stand firm in the truth and expose the delusions that arise in our midst.

Through sound teaching and preaching, led by pastors and spiritual leaders committed to the truth, the church can become a safe haven from false doctrine and a place of growth and strength in the faith.

As we deepen our knowledge of the Word of God, we are enabled to recognize the false prophecies that seek to lead us away from the path of truth. Spiritual watchfulness is essential to spot these deceivers, whose aim is to weaken our faith and trust in the Lord.

ROOTS OF DISAPPOINTMENT

To understand the magnitude of the problem of false prophets, it is essential to investigate their origins and causes, as well as understanding how deception can infiltrate our communities. In this chapter, we will delve into the scriptures and Church history, seeking to identify the roots of deception and the challenges it poses to believers.

7

The Origin of Deceit

To understand the roots of the deception propagated by false prophets, it is crucial to go back to the beginning of human history, to the account of the fall of man in the book of Genesis.

In Genesis chapter 3, we find the narrative of the deceiving serpent who, under the guise of cunning, led Eve to doubt God's words and to give in to the temptation to eat the forbidden fruit. This fall of man introduced sin into the world and marked the beginning of a battle between truth and lies, a struggle that continues to this day.

Genesis 3:1-6 "Now the serpent was more subtil than any beast of the field which the Lord God had made. And he said unto the woman, Has God said, Ye shall not eat of every tree of the garden? If you eat of it, your eyes will be opened, and you will be like God, knowing good and evil." When the woman saw that the tree was good for food, that it was pleasant to the eyes and that the tree is desirable to make one wise, she took some of its fruit and ate, and gave it to her husband, and he ate."

The cunning and manipulation used by the serpent in this early episode of human history are characteristics that are also evident in the false prophets that arise throughout the ages.

They use persuasion and deception to lead people away from the truth and turn their hearts away from the Lord.

Prophetic Alerts

Throughout the Old Testament, we find numerous warnings and prophecies about the presence of false prophets among God's people. Through genuine prophets, God warned the people of the danger of being led astray by those who spread false messages.

Jeremiah 14:14 "The Lord said to me, The prophets prophesy falsely in my name; I never sent them, nor commanded them, nor spoke to them; false vision, divination, vanity and the deceitfulness of their heart are what they prophesy to you."

In this passage, Jeremiah denounces the false prophets who acted in the name of God, but whose words were the fruit of their own illusions and heart deceit. They deceived the people, leading them to believe in false hopes and groundless revelations.

Ezekiel 13:3 "Thus says the Lord God: Woe to the foolish prophets who follow their own spirit and have seen nothing!"

Ezekiel also sharply criticizes prophets who acted under the influence of their own spirits rather than truly listening to God's voice. These prophets misled the people with their visions and empty prophecies.

False Prophets in Israel

The history of the people of Israel is full of examples of false prophets who emerged to deceive the people and divert their allegiance from the true God.

In the book of 1 Kings, we find the narrative of one of the best known false prophets in biblical history: Hananiah. He contradicted the words of the prophet Jeremiah and claimed that the Lord would free the people of Israel from Babylonian bondage in just two years.

1 Kings 28:10-11 "Then Hananiah the prophet took the yoke from the neck of the prophet Jeremiah and broke it.

However, Hananiah's words were lies, and God revealed to Jeremiah that this false prophet would be punished for his lies.

Jeremiah 28:15-17 "Then said Jeremiah the prophet unto Hananiah the prophet, Hear now, Hananiah: The LORD hath not sent thee, but thou hast caused this people to trust in lies. Therefore thus saith the LORD, Behold, I will cast thee out from off the face of the earth: thou shalt die this year, because

10

thou hast preached rebellion against the LORD. And Hananiah the prophet died in the same year, in the seventh month."

This narrative demonstrates how false prophets can lead people to believe lies and how their actions have serious consequences.

Jesus' Warning Against False Prophets

In the New Testament, Jesus Christ also issued scathing warnings against false prophets that would arise after His departure. He warned His disciples to be vigilant and discern these deceptive figures.

Matthew 24:24-25 "For false Christs and false prophets will arise, performing great signs and wonders to deceive, if possible, the very elect. Behold, I told you beforehand."

In this passage, Jesus predicts the coming of false Christs and false prophets, endowed with abilities to perform impressive signs and miracles, in order to lead astray even God's elect.

The Lack of Discernment

One of the roots of the deception of false prophets is the lack of spiritual discernment in the people. The absence of an intimate relationship with God and a shallow understanding of Scripture can make believers vulnerable to manipulation and deception.

Hosea 4:6 "My people are destroyed for lack of knowledge.

In this passage, the prophet Hosea laments the destruction of the people for lack of knowledge. Knowledge of the Word of God is essential for strengthening faith and discerning true teachings.

The Quest for Signs and Wonders

Another root of the false prophets' disappointment is in the excessive search for signs and wonders, to the detriment of the search for the true relationship with God.

Matthew 12:39 "But he answered them, An evil and adulterous generation seeks a sign; but no sign shall be given it, save that of Jonah the prophet."

People are often attracted to false prophets because of the miracles and wonders they perform. However, Jesus warned that true faith is not based on spectacular miracles, but on trust and obedience to God's will.

The Corruption of the Human Heart

Finally, the roots of deception can also be found in the very fallen nature of the human heart. The inclination towards sin and rebellion against God make people more susceptible to the deceptions of false prophets.

2 Timothy 4:3-4 "For the time will come when they will not endure sound doctrine; but according to their own desires, they will heap up for themselves teachers, as if they had itching ears; and they will refuse to listen to the truth, and will be turned aside to fables."

Paul, in his letter to Timothy, predicted that many would seek to hear only what pleases them and would depart from sound doctrine. This departure from the truth would open space for the influence of false prophets, who would take advantage of human greed and desires to deceive and manipulate.

As we investigate the roots of the deception promoted by false prophets, it becomes clear that this problem is not something new, but an issue that has accompanied humanity since its fall. The Scriptures, from the Old Testament to the New Testament, alert us to the presence of these deceptive figures and the importance of discerning their messages and actions.

The constant search for knowledge of the Word of God, combined with an intimate relationship with the Lord, is essential to strengthen our faith and protect us against false teachings. Spiritual discernment, guided by the Holy Spirit, enables us to identify false prophets and reject their lies.

THE SIGNS OF FALSE PROPHETS

Identifying false prophets is an essential task to protect our Christian faith and community. In this chapter, we will analyze the characteristic signs of these deceivers, understanding their strategies and discerning the true light that should guide us. The Scriptures provide us with precious guidance on how to recognize these misleading figures, so that we are not led adrift by their false doctrines and baseless revelations.

14

One of the main signs of false prophets is their contradiction to the Word of God revealed in the Scriptures. They present teachings that clash with the principles and commandments taught by God. Instead of promoting truth and righteousness, their messages lead to error and distortion of the Word.

Jeremiah 23:16-17 "Thus saith the Lord of hosts, Hearken not to the words of the prophets which prophesy among you: they teach you vanities, and speak from the strength of their own heart, not from the mouth of the Lord.

Here, the Lord warns against prophets who proclaim empty words, born from their own hearts and not from the Lord. They comfort sinners in their rebellion, promising them peace and security even when they are straying from God's ways.

Deceptive Signs and Wonders

False prophets often seek to impress people with deceptive signs and miracles in order to attract followers and gain their trust. However, these signs can be illusory and do not come from God.

Matthew 24:24 "For false Christs and false prophets will arise, performing great signs and wonders to deceive, if possible, the very elect."

15

In this passage, Jesus predicts the coming of false Christs and false prophets who will work amazing signs and miracles to deceive, if possible, even God's elect. This warning highlights the importance of spiritual discernment in order not to be deceived by apparent displays of supernatural power.

Search for Personal Interests

False prophets often act out of self-interest, seeking their own benefits, such as riches, fame, and power. Their motives are self-centered rather than the will of God or the welfare of the people they address.

Micah 3:11 "Their rulers judge for bribes, their priests teach for profit, and their prophets divine for money. Yet they lean on the Lord and say, 'The Lord is with us. No harm will befall us.'"

In this passage, Micah denounces corrupt leaders who act in their own interests, judging based on bribes, priests teaching for profit, and prophets guessing for money. They may even call on the name of the Lord, but their actions reveal their true selfish motive.

Teachings Contrary to the Gospel

False prophets can present teachings that deviate from the essence of the Gospel, denying crucial aspects of the Christian faith and inducing people to adopt erroneous doctrines.

2 Pedro 2:1-3 "So also false teachers will arise among you, who will secretly introduce destructive heresies, even to the point of denying the Sovereign Lord who bought them, bringing upon themselves sudden destruction. And many will follow their licentious practices, and because of them the way of truth will be infamous; their destruction does not sleep."

In this passage, Peter warns against false teachers who introduce destructive heresies and deny the Lord who rescued them. They take advantage of the spiritual weakness of many to lead them to follow licentious practices and, moved by avarice, they exploit their victims with fictitious words. The warning is clear: your actions will have consequences and your destruction will not take long.

The Glorification of False Prophets

A common characteristic of false prophets is the relentless pursuit of personal recognition and glory. They strive to gain fame and prominence among their followers by promoting themselves as charismatic and spiritual figures.

17

Matthew 23:5-7 "They practice all their actions in order to be seen by men; for they lengthen their phylacteries and lengthen the fringes of their garments; they love the place of honor at banquets and the first seats in the synagogues; and to be saluted in the marketplaces and to be called teachers of men."

Jesus denounces false teachers who seek to show off before people, wanting to be seen and recognized for their supposed spiritual actions. They seek honor and praise from others rather than seeking to please God in humility and service.

Absence of Fruits of the Spirit

An effective way to discern false prophets is to observe their fruit, that is, the result of their actions and teachings. The lack of manifestation of the fruits of the Holy Spirit in their lives is a clear sign that their messages are not from God.

Galatians 5:22-23 "But the fruit of the Spirit is love, joy, peace, longsuffering, gentleness, goodness, faithfulness, gentleness, self-control. Against these things there is no law."

True prophets are known by the fruits of the Spirit they manifest in their lives. If someone's teachings and actions do not line up with love, kindness, peace and other fruits of the Spirit, it is an indication that that person may be a false prophet.

Appeal to Emotional Experience

False prophets often appeal to people's emotional experience, using manipulation and exaggeration to create an intense emotional atmosphere in their meetings and events. They can emphasize supposed manifestations of the Holy Spirit, causing people to react emotionally without solid foundation in the Word of God.

Ephesians 4:14 "That we should be no more children, tossed to and fro, and carried about with every wind of doctrine, by the craftiness of men, by their cunning craftiness in deceiving."

Paul warns the Christians in Ephesus of the importance of growing in the maturity of the faith, lest they be easily tossed about by every wind of doctrine, which includes appealing to emotional experience without biblical foundation.

Life inconsistency

False prophets often exhibit inconsistency between their words and their actions, which reveals a lack of integrity and a divided heart.

Matthew 23:27-28 "Woe to you, scribes and Pharisees, hypocrites!

Jesus rebukes the scribes and Pharisees for their hypocrisy and wickedness, highlighting the inconsistency between their outward appearance and their true inward condition. False prophets who behave in this way reveal their lack of integrity and sincerity.

Manipulation and Control

False prophets can use manipulative tactics to control their congregations and prevent people from questioning their actions and teachings.

2 Pedro 2:18 "For, uttering boastful words of vanity, they entice with carnal lusts, by their licentiousness, those who were about to flee from those who walk in error."

Peter describes false teachers who use vain and boastful words to entice and manipulate those who are about to escape their deceptions. These false prophets exploit human weaknesses and carnal passions to keep people under their control.

Lack of Accountability

False prophets often avoid accountability and resist any form of criticism or correction. They seek to insulate themselves from questioning voices in order to maintain their hold on their followers.

1 John 4:1 "Beloved, believe not every spirit, but try the spirits whether they are of God, because many false prophets are gone out into the world."

John exhorts us to test the spirits to discern whether they are from God. False prophets often resist scrutiny and avoid being tested, which is a telltale sign of their deceptive nature.

Identifying false prophets is a vital responsibility for every Christian who seeks true faith and a relationship with God. Through knowledge of the Scriptures and spiritual discernment, we can recognize the hallmarks of these deceivers and guard our faith against their wiles.

False prophets contradict the Word of God, use deceptive signs and miracles, seek personal interests, promote teachings contrary to the Gospel, seek personal glory, do not manifest the fruits of the Spirit, appeal to emotional experience, exhibit inconsistency of life, manipulate and seek to avoid accountability. By being alert to these signs, we can resist its temptations and stand firm in the true light that is Christ, our Lord and Savior.

THE TRUE WORD OF GOD

Amidst the turmoil of false revelations and the deceptions of false prophets, relying on the true Word of God is essential to strengthen our faith and discernment. In this chapter, we will deepen our understanding of the source of true wisdom and the importance of discerning the authentic teachings contained in Holy Scripture and Church tradition. By examining biblical passages and understanding the role of Scripture in our Christian life, we will be prepared to resist lies and embrace the truth that leads us to solid and genuine faith.

22

The Authority of Scripture

The Word of God is the basis and foundation of the Christian faith. The Holy Bible is recognized as God's written revelation to humanity, inspired by the Holy Spirit and transcribed by God's chosen men.

2 Timothy 3:16-17 "All Scripture is inspired by God and useful for teaching, for reproof, for correction and for training in righteousness, so that the man of God may be complete, equipped for every good work."

In this passage, the apostle Paul emphasizes that all Scripture is inspired by God and has a clear purpose: to teach, rebuke, correct and educate in righteousness. The Word of God is a compass for our spiritual life, guiding us in our actions and decisions, preparing us to live according to the divine will.

The authority of Scripture is unquestionable, and it is through it that we can discern truth from false teachings and misleading revelations.

The Transforming Power of the Word

Hebrews 4:12 "For the Word of God is living, and powerful, and sharper than any two-edged sword, piercing even to the division of soul and spirit, and of joints and marrow, and is able to discern the thoughts and intents of the heart."

The Word of God is living and powerful, able to penetrate deep into our soul and spirit, revealing our innermost thoughts and intentions. It has the power to transform our lives, shape our character, and lead us into deeper communion with God.

Thus, by holding fast to the Word of God, we are able to clearly discern authentic teachings and avoid being deceived by false prophets who propagate lies.

The Quest for Divine Wisdom

True wisdom comes from God, and it is through the Word that we find guidance for our daily lives.

Proverbs 2:6 "For the Lord gives wisdom, and out of his mouth comes knowledge and understanding."

True wisdom is given by the Lord Himself. It does not originate in human teachings or worldly philosophies, but from the Word of God. As we delve into the Scriptures and seek to understand God's will for our lives, we are filled with true wisdom that enables us to discern what is right and make decisions in line with His will.

The Firmness of Biblical Teachings

Matthew 7:24-25 "Therefore everyone who hears these words of mine and does them will be likened to a wise man who built his house on the rock. And the rain came down, the torrents ran, the winds blew and beat against that house, which did not fall, because it was built on the rock."

Jesus compares the one who hears and practices His words to a wise man who builds his house on the rock. When life's storms arise, this house stands firm and unshakable because it has a solid foundation. Likewise, when we base our lives on the Scriptures and live according to their teachings, we are able to face life's challenges and trials with steadfastness and trust in God.

The Admonition against the Distortion of the Word

Pedro 3:15-16 "But sanctify Christ as Lord in your hearts, always being prepared to give an answer to everyone who asks you to give the reason for the hope that is in you, yet doing so with meekness and fear, with a good conscience, so that those who speak against you may be ashamed who speak ill of your good dealings in Christ."

Peter exhorts us to be always ready to give a reason for the hope that is in us, but this must be done with meekness, fear, and a good conscience. It is essential that we not distort God's Word to suit personal interests or to promote erroneous doctrines. Rather, we should diligently study the Scriptures, seeking a correct understanding of biblical teachings and sharing them humbly and respectfully.

The Guidance of the Holy Spirit

Full understanding of God's Word requires the guidance of the Holy Spirit. It is He who teaches us the truth and leads us to a correct understanding of the Scriptures.

1 Corinthians 2:12-14 "Now we have not received the spirit of the world, but the Spirit who is from God, that we may know what has been freely given to us by God. These things we also speak, not in words taught by human wisdom but taught by the Spirit, comparing spiritual things with spiritual. Now the natural man does not accept the things of the Spirit of God, because they are foolishness to him;

Paul points out that as Christians we have received the Spirit of God so that we may know what has been freely given to us. It is through the guidance of the Holy Spirit that we discern the spiritual teachings contained in the Scriptures, and the natural man, that is, he who does not have the Spirit of God, cannot fully understand them.

Thus, as we study the Word of God, we must pray and seek the guidance of the Holy Spirit, allowing Him to enlighten us and reveal the truth amid the diverse interpretations and voices present in the world.

The Tradition of the Church

In addition to the Scriptures, Church tradition also plays an important role in understanding authentic teachings. Tradition refers to the set of teachings, practices, and doctrines handed down over the centuries by Church fathers and faithful Christians.

2 Thessalonians 2:15 "So then, brethren, stand firm and hold the traditions which you were taught, whether by word or our epistle."

Paul encourages Christians to keep the traditions they have been taught, whether orally or in writing. Tradition, along with Scripture, is a pillar of the Christian faith, providing a solid foundation for our understanding of the teachings of Christ and the apostles.

It is important to emphasize that tradition is not an addition or replacement of the Scriptures, but rather an interpretation and explanation of the truth contained in them. Church tradition helps to preserve and transmit the apostolic teaching from generation to generation, ensuring the continuity of the Christian faith.

The Unity of the Body of Christ

1 Corinthians 1:10 "I beseech you, brethren, by the name of our Lord Jesus Christ, that you all speak the same thing and that there be no divisions among you, but that you be completely united, in the same mental disposition and in the same opinion."

The Word of God and the tradition of the Church are designed to unite the Body of Christ, the Church, in one common faith and frame of mind. Unity among Christians is a powerful testimony to the transforming power of God's Word and its practical application in our lives.

It is through the Word and tradition that we find the foundation for unity and spiritual growth in our journey of faith.

The Call to Spiritual Maturity

Hebrews 5:12-14 "For indeed, when you ought to be teachers, in view of the elapsed time, you again need someone to teach you again what are the elementary principles of the oracles of God; thus you have become as needing milk and not solid food. Now everyone who feeds on milk is inexperienced in the word of righteousness, because he is a child. but also evil."

The Word of God is compared to spiritual food that nourishes our faith and leads us to spiritual growth and maturity. Just as a child needs milk in its initial phase, Christians also need to start feeding on the Word to grow in faith.

However, it is important to progress in understanding the Word and to mature spiritually. Only those who exercise their faculties to discern good from evil can clearly recognize the authentic teachings of God's Word.

The Supremacy of Christ and His Word

Colossians 1:17-18 "And he is before all things, and through him all things hold together. He is the head of the body, the church. He is the beginning, the firstborn from among the dead, that in all things he might have the primacy."

Jesus Christ is the center and foundation of our faith. He is the incarnate Word, and his supremacy is indisputable. It is through His Word that we find the true light that guides us through the darkness of false revelations and teachings.

The true Word of God, expressed in Holy Scripture and Church tradition, is our compass and anchor amid the storms of deceit and falsehood. She is alive and powerful, capable of transforming our lives and molding our character according to the divine will.

By deepening our understanding of the authority of the Scriptures, the transforming power of the Word, the search for divine wisdom, the firmness of biblical teachings, the admonition against the distortion of the Word, the guidance of the Holy Spirit, the tradition of the Church, the unity of the Body of Christ, the call to spiritual maturity and the supremacy of Christ and His Word, we will be prepared to face the challenges posed by false prophets and remain firm in the truth that sets us free and leads us to a genuine and full faith in God.

THE HUMILITY OF A TRUE SERVANT

The quest for recognition and power is one of the hallmarks of false prophets and deceivers. However, humility is an essential virtue for a true servant of God. In this chapter, we will explore the importance of humility in the Christian life, contrasting it with the pride and vanity that can easily permeate the conduct of those who deviate from the true path of faith. Through biblical passages, we will learn about the example of humility left by Jesus Christ and how this virtue should be cultivated in our lives as disciples of Christ.

31

Humility Exemplified by Jesus

One of the most striking and humbling figures in the Bible is Jesus Christ, the Son of God who became man to save mankind. He left a concrete example of how a true servant should be humble.

Philippians 2:5-8 "Have this mind in you that was also in Christ Jesus, who, existing in the form of God, did not consider equality with God a thing to be grasped, but made himself of no reputation, taking the form of a servant, being made in the likeness of men; and being recognized in human form, he humbled himself, becoming obedient to death, even death on a cross."

In this passage, Paul highlights the humility of Christ in emptying Himself of His divine glory and taking the form of a servant, becoming in the likeness of men. He humbly obeyed even to the death on the cross, demonstrating an unparalleled love and dedication for humanity.

By following the example of humility left by Jesus, we understand that true greatness is not in seeking recognition or power, but in serving others with love and selflessness.

The Call to Humility in the Teachings of Jesus

Jesus repeatedly emphasized the importance of humility in His teachings, inviting His disciples to abandon vanity and pride and become servants to one another.

Matthew 18:3-4 "Truly I say to you, unless you convert and become like children, you will by no means enter the kingdom of heaven. Therefore, whoever humbles himself like this child, he is the greatest in the kingdom of heaven."

In this passage, Jesus emphasizes the need to become like children in terms of humility. Childhood humility is characterized by the absence of pride, ambition and desire for recognition. Jesus invites His followers to abandon selfish attitudes and humble themselves, for this is how they become the greatest in the kingdom of heaven.

Humility as a Key to Exaltation

The Bible teaches us that humility is a virtue that God exalts and rewards. Those who humble themselves before the Lord are honored by Him.

James 4:10 "Humble yourselves in the presence of the Lord, and he will lift you up."

James emphasizes that the right attitude before God is humility. Those who humble themselves in the presence of the Lord will be exalted by Him, that is, they will be honored and elevated by God.

This passage underscores the importance of placing ourselves in a position of submission and dependence on God, recognizing that all honor and exaltation comes from Him and not from our own efforts.

The Prayer of the Humble Publican

Jesus told a parable about two men who went to the temple to pray, a Pharisee and a publican (tax collector). The Pharisee prayed with pride, exalting himself before God, while the publican prayed with humility, acknowledging his sinfulness.

Lucas 18:13-14 "But the publican, standing far off, dared not even raise his eyes to heaven, but beat his breast, saying, O God, be merciful to me, a sinner! I tell you, this man went down to his house justified rather than the other; for everyone who exalts himself will be humbled, but he who humbles himself will be exalted."

In this parable, Jesus teaches about the importance of humility in prayer. The publican, by recognizing his sinful condition, was justified before God, while the Pharisee, full of pride and self-justification, was not heard by God.

The lesson is clear: humility opens the way for divine grace and mercy in our lives.

God Resists the Proud

The Bible warns us about the danger of pride and the fact that God resists the proud.

James 4:6 "God, however, gives greater grace; for he says, God resists the proud, but gives grace to the humble."

James highlights that God grants greater grace to the humble, but resists the proud, that is, the proud and arrogant. Those who exalt themselves before God find barriers to receiving divine grace, while the humble are graced with His goodness and mercy.

The Example of John the Baptist

John the Baptist, the prophet who prepared the way for Jesus Christ, is another outstanding example of humility in the Bible.

John 3:30 "He needs to increase and I need to decrease."

In this passage, John summarizes his mission as the forerunner of Christ. He understands that his own importance is secondary to the greatness of Jesus. John puts himself in a position of humility, recognizing that his task is to decrease so that Jesus can grow.

This example shows how humility is linked to exalting the name of Jesus and submitting to His lordship.

Jesus' Service Attitude

Humility is intrinsically linked to the attitude of service exemplified by Jesus. He came into the world not to be served, but to serve and to give His life a ransom for many.

Marcos 10:45 "For the Son of Man did not come to be served, but to serve and to give his life as a ransom for many."

Jesus, as the Son of God, could have demanded honor and recognition, but he chose a life of humble service, showing us the true meaning of love and giving to others.

This attitude of service is a model for all of His followers. The true servant of God must also place himself in the service of others, without seeking personal honor or reward.

The Call to Humility in Living with the Brothers

Humility is fundamental in living with brothers in Christ. Paul exhorts Christians to walk humbly, considering others better than themselves.

Philippians 2:3-4 "Do nothing through strife or vainglory, but in humility consider others better than yourselves. Do not look each to his own, but each also to the things of others."

In this passage, Paul highlights the importance of acting in humility and considering others better than ourselves. It means putting the welfare of others above our own, serving and loving them selflessly.

Humility in living with brothers and sisters strengthens communion and testifies to the love of Christ in our lives.

Humility as a Key to Restoration

Humility is also the key to spiritual restoration and healing.

2 Chronicles 7:14 "If my people, who are called by my name, will humble themselves, and pray, and seek my face, and turn from their wicked ways, then will I hear from heaven, will forgive their sin, and will heal their land."

In this passage, God makes a promise conditioned on the humility of His people. If God's people will humble themselves, seek His face, and turn from their evil ways, then He will hear, forgive, and bring healing and restoration.

This passage shows that humility is the starting point for experiencing grace and divine restoration in our lives and in our community.

The Wisdom That Comes from Humility

Humility is the source of true and genuine wisdom.

Proverbs 11:2 "When pride comes, dishonor will also come, but with the humble is wisdom."

Proverbs points out that pride leads to dishonor, while wisdom is present in humble hearts. Those who remain humble before God are enabled to see the true wisdom that comes from Him.

Humility is an essential virtue for the true servant of God. It is exemplified by Jesus Christ, who emptied himself of his divine glory to serve humanity. Through biblical passages, we learn about the importance of humility as a key to exaltation and restoration, and how it is intrinsically linked to the attitude of service and socializing with brothers in Christ.

By cultivating humility in our lives, abandoning pride and vanity, we will be following in the footsteps of our Lord and living a life of service and love for others. Humility leads us to true wisdom and brings us closer to the heart of God, allowing us to experience the fullness of His grace and mercy. Therefore, may we daily strive for humility, allowing it to be a hallmark of our Christian witness and an expression of God's love in us.

CLINGING TO GENUINE FAITH

Genuine faith is a powerful protection against the onslaughts of false prophets. In this chapter, we will address the importance of strengthening our personal relationship with God, rooting ourselves in prayer, devotion and living the sacraments, in order to avoid falling into the traps of falsehood.

The Foundation of Faith: Belief in God

Genuine faith has as its central foundation to believe in God, His love and His Word.

Hebrews 11:6 "Now without faith it is impossible to please him; for he who approaches God must believe that he exists and that he is a rewarder of those who diligently seek him."

In this passage, the author of Hebrews emphasizes that it is impossible to please God without faith. Those who wish to approach God must believe in His existence and His character as a rewarder of those who seek Him.

Genuine faith begins with believing that God is real, that He is good, and that He wants to have a relationship with us. This belief drives us to seek an intimate relationship with Him, which is essential to guard against false revelations and misleading teachings.

The Importance of Constant Prayer

Prayer is one of the fundamental practices of the Christian faith. It connects us with God, strengthens our fellowship with Him, and helps us discern His will for our lives.

1 Thessalonians 5:17 "Pray without ceasing."

Paul exhorts us to pray without ceasing, that is, to maintain an attitude of constant communication with God. Prayer is a way of expressing our dependence on God, our gratitude, and our longing. It is also a way for us to seek divine guidance, asking for discernment to avoid falling into the traps of false prophets.

By cultivating a life of prayer, we strengthen our genuine faith and are better able to distinguish God's voice from the enemy's lies.

Devotion as an Expression of Love for God

Devotion is another important practice for strengthening our genuine faith. It consists of dedicating a special time to worship God, meditate on His Word and render Him praises.

Salmo 119:105 "Your word is a lamp to my feet, a light to my path."

Psalm 119 emphasizes the importance of God's Word as a lamp that lights our way. By dedicating ourselves to reading and meditating on the Scriptures, we find guidance and insight to avoid being deceived by false revelations and doctrines.

Furthermore, devotion is an expression of love and reverence for God. As we take the time to seek Him in prayer and the

42

Scriptures, we demonstrate that He is the center of our lives and that we are willing to listen to Him and obey His teachings.

Experiencing the Sacraments as a Source of Grace

Sacraments are channels of grace instituted by Jesus Christ to strengthen our faith and unite us with Him in a special way.

Matthew 28:19-20 "Therefore go and make disciples of all nations, baptizing them in the name of the Father and of the Son and of the Holy Spirit, teaching them to observe all that I have commanded you. And, lo, I am with you always, even to the end of the age."

In this passage, known as the Great Commission, Jesus instructs His disciples to baptize in the name of the Trinity and teach them to keep His ordinances. Baptism is a sacrament that symbolizes our identification with Christ in His death, burial, and resurrection, and it marks the beginning of our lives as disciples of Christ.

Another important sacrament is the Eucharist, in which we partake of the body and blood of Christ, strengthening our communion with Him and with the Church.

As we experience the sacraments with genuine faith, we are nourished and strengthened by God's grace, which enables us to resist the temptations and pitfalls of false prophets.

Knowledge of the Scriptures as a Shield Against Deception

Knowing the Scriptures is an effective way to guard against the deception of false prophets.

Matthew 22:29 "Jesus, however, answered them: You err, not knowing the Scriptures nor the power of God."

In this passage, Jesus rebukes the Sadducees for their error, the result of their lack of knowledge of the Scriptures and the power of God. Knowledge of the Word of God is fundamental to discerning true teachings from false ones.

When we dig deeper into the Scriptures and diligently study the truths revealed by God, we become more sensitive to the lies and distortions that false prophets propagate. The Bible is the lamp that lights our paths and guides us to true wisdom and discernment.

The Work of the Holy Spirit in Discerning the Truth

The Holy Ghost plays a key role in our discernment of truth and the strengthening of our genuine faith.

1 John 2:27 "As for you, the anointing you received from him abides in you, and you have no need for anyone to teach you; but as his anointing teaches you about all things, and is true and not false, abide in him, just as it also taught you."

John points out that the anointing of the Holy Spirit in us teaches us about all things and is true. This anointing enables us to discern the truth and recognize the lies and falsehoods that may come our way.

It is important, therefore, that we cultivate an intimate relationship with the Holy Spirit, allowing Him to guide us and reveal the truth of God's heart.

The Spiritual Combat in Genuine Faith

Genuine faith is the target of constant attacks from the spiritual enemy. The apostle Peter warns of the need to be vigilant and firm in our faith.

1 Pedro 5:8-9 "Be sober, be vigilant. The devil, your adversary, walks around like a roaring lion looking for someone to devour; resist him firm in the faith, certain that sufferings equal to yours are being fulfilled in your brotherhood spread throughout the world."

Peter warns that the devil, our adversary, seeks to devour us like a roaring lion. Resisting the enemy requires steadfast faith, trust in God, and knowledge of His Word.

Spiritual warfare is a reality for every Christian, and genuine faith equips us to meet the enemy's wiles with the spiritual armor provided by God (Ephesians 6:10-18).

Communion with the Community of Faith

Communion with the faith community is an essential part of genuine faith. The Church is a united body in Christ, and fellowship with other Christians strengthens our faith and helps us discern truth.

Hebrews 10:24-25 "And let us consider one another to spur one another on to love and good works, not forsaking the congregation of ourselves, as some have the habit of admonishing, and so much the more as you see the Day approaching."

The author of Hebrews encourages believers to come together and stir one another up to love and good works. Fellowship with fellow believers provides mutual support, encouragement, and correction, helping us to grow in our genuine faith.

Through fellowship with the Church, we have access to solid teachings, loving correction, and the support we need to withstand the attacks of false prophets.

Firm Faith in Times of Trials

Genuine faith is tested in times of trial and adversity. Firmness in faith is an indication of our trust in God, even in the face of difficulties.

James 1:2-4 "Count it all joy, my brethren, when you pass through various trials, knowing that the trial of your faith, once confirmed, produces perseverance. Now, perseverance must have complete action, so that you may be perfect and complete, lacking nothing."

James encourages believers to consider trials as a source of joy, as they produce perseverance and maturity in the faith. Firmness of faith amidst trials is a powerful testimony of our trust in God and our genuine faith.

The Example of Faith of the Heroes of the Faith

Hebrews chapter 11 is known as the "roll of the heroes of faith". In it, the author highlights several biblical characters who stood out for their genuine and unshakable faith.

Hebrews 11:1 "Now faith is the assurance of things hoped for, the conviction of things not seen."

Hebrews 11:6 "Indeed, without faith it is impossible to please God, for he who approaches God must believe that he exists and that he becomes a rewarder of those who seek him."

Hebrews chapter 11 presents an impressive list of men and women who, by faith, accomplished great works and faced adversity with courage and determination.

The example of faith of these heroes of faith inspires us to cultivate genuine faith in our lives, clinging to God in all circumstances and resisting the onslaughts of false prophets.

Genuine faith is a powerful protection against the snares of false prophets. Strengthening our personal relationship with God, rooting ourselves in prayer, devotion and experiencing the sacraments, knowing and meditating on the Scriptures, allowing the work of the Holy Spirit in us, resisting the enemy in spiritual combat, seeking communion with the community of faith, being firm in faith in times of trial and learning from the example of faith of the heroes of faith, are essential elements to strengthen our genuine faith and remain firm in the truth of God.

By cultivating a solid and authentic faith, we will be able to discern and reject the deceptive teachings of false prophets, remaining faithful to the true gospel of Christ and witnessing His light in a world full of darkness and falsehood. May we diligently and humbly seek to deepen our genuine faith by living it practically and consistently in all areas of our lives.

THE RESPONSIBILITY OF THE FAITHFUL

We are all called to be guardians of the faith and to watch over the doctrinal integrity of the Church. In this chapter, we will discuss the responsibility of the faithful to denounce deceptive practices, protecting our religious community from the dangers posed by false prophets.

The Warning Against False Prophets

Since biblical times, God has warned His people about false prophets and their deceptive practices. The Bible exhorts us to be vigilant and to discern God's true message from that which is distorted by false teachers.

Matthew 7:15 "Beware of false prophets, which come to you in sheep's clothing, but inwardly they are ravening wolves."

Jesus warned his disciples to beware of false prophets, who come in sheep's clothing but have malicious intent, like ravening wolves. This warning highlights the importance of being attentive to the teachings and revelations that are propagated by religious leaders, verifying that they are aligned with the Scriptures and with the true message of Christ.

The Responsibility of Confronting Deception

The responsibility for confronting deception and denouncing deceptive practices rests with the entire body of believers. The Bible encourages us to be courageous and not remain silent in the face of falsehoods that threaten the community of faith.

Ephesians 5:11 "And have no fellowship with the unfruitful works of darkness, but rather reprove them."

Paul exhorts believers not to be partakers of the unfruitful works of darkness, but to reprove them. This means that we must not turn a blind eye to deceitful practices, but must bring them to light and reject them on the basis of the truth revealed in the Word of God.

When we remain silent in the face of error, we allow error to spread and negatively affect the faith and life of the community of believers. Therefore, the responsibility to confront deception is a matter of protecting and preserving genuine faith.

The Quest for Wisdom and Discernment

To fulfill our responsibility to discern and denounce deception, we need to seek the wisdom and discernment that come from God.

Proverbs 2:3-6 "If you cry out for discernment and lift up your voice for understanding, if you search for it like silver and search for it as for hidden treasures, then you will understand the fear of the LORD and find the knowledge of God. For the LORD gives wisdom; from his mouth come knowledge and understanding."

The Proverbs teach us that we need to seek wisdom and understanding as if we were searching for precious treasures.

Wisdom comes from God and is acquired through the fear of the Lord and the knowledge of His Word.

When we are wise and discern the truth, we are able to identify deceptive practices and protect our faith community from the snares of false prophets.

The Importance of Unity in Truth

The responsibility to expose deception is also linked to maintaining unity in truth within the faith community.

Ephesians 4:3 "By striving diligently to preserve the unity of the Spirit in the bond of peace."

Paul exhorts believers to strive diligently to preserve the unity of the Spirit in the bond of peace. This means that when we confront deception, we must do so with love, humility and a desire for restoration, seeking to build and strengthen the community of faith.

Confronting deception without love and compassion can lead to unnecessary divisions and strife within the church. Therefore, it is fundamental that the responsibility to denounce deception be exercised based on love and the search for true unity in Christ.

Paul's Example and the Defense of the Faith

The apostle Paul is an inspiring example of how to face deception and defend genuine faith. In his epistles he frequently rebuked deceitful practices and false doctrines that threatened the integrity of the Christian faith.

Galatians 1:8-9 "But even if we, or even an angel from heaven, preach a gospel to you that exceeds what we have preached to you, let him be accursed. So, as we have said, and now I repeat, if anyone preaches a gospel to you that exceeds what you received, let him be accursed."

In this passage, Paul emphasizes the seriousness of defending genuine faith. He warns believers not to accept any message or teaching that goes beyond what was preached by him and the other apostles.

Paul's attitude reflects his concern for doctrinal purity and the protection of the church against false prophets and distorted teachings.

The Denunciation of the False Teaching in Corinth

Another notable example of Paul's zeal for doctrinal integrity is his approach to false teaching in the Corinthian church.

2 Corinthians 11:13-15 "For such are false apostles, deceitful workers, transforming themselves into the apostles of Christ.

Paul denounces false apostles who masquerade as messengers of Christ but who are really deceitful workers.

He warns the church about the possibility of Satan transforming himself into an angel of light and his followers into ministers of righteousness.

Paul's denunciation in Corinth shows the importance of identifying and confronting false teachers in order to protect the community of faith against deceptive practices and their harmful consequences.

Love and Truth in Confrontation

The responsibility to expose deceit must be exercised in love and truth. The Bible teaches us to speak the truth in love, seeking the edification and restoration of those involved in deceit.

Ephesians 4:15 "Rather, following the truth in love, let us grow in everything into him who is the head, Christ."

Paul emphasizes the importance of following the truth in love, growing in everything in Christ who is the head. This means that our responsibility to denounce deception must be rooted in a desire to bring people to a greater knowledge of Christ and His truth.

The truth must be spoken with compassion and respect, avoiding hasty judgments or condemnations. The goal is always restoration and reconciliation, not estrangement or division.

Wisdom in Identifying False Prophets

To fulfill our responsibility to protect the community of faith against false prophets, we need to be aware of the distinctive signs that identify them.

Matthew 24:24 "For false Christs and false prophets will arise, performing great signs and wonders to deceive, if possible, the very elect."

Jesus warned that false Christs and false prophets would arise who would perform great signs and wonders to deceive, if possible, the very elect. The presence of miracles and wonders is no guarantee of divine authenticity, as the enemy can also perform misleading signs.

Therefore, our wisdom in identifying false prophets is rooted in the Word of God and knowledge of His teachings. We must seek discernment and the guidance of the Holy Spirit lest we be deceived by deceptive practices that may masquerade as manifestations of divine power.

Confrontation in the Quest for Restoration

The responsibility of confronting deception is not only to denounce but also to seek restoration for those who engage in deceptive practices.

Galatians 6:1 "Brothers, if a man is caught in any trespass, you who are spiritual restore such a one in a spirit of gentleness; and take heed to yourself, lest you also be tempted."

Paul instructs the brethren to approach in a spirit of gentleness those who are caught in some offense. Confrontation must be guided by care and concern for the restoration of the individual.

We must remember that we are all prone to temptations and weaknesses, and an attitude of gentleness and compassion is essential to helping those involved repent and turn to the true faith.

The Importance of Solid and Disciplined Teaching

An effective way to protect the community of faith against false prophets is through sound and disciplined teaching.

Tito 1:9 "Clinging to the faithful word which is according to doctrine, so that he may have power both to exhort by sound teaching and to convince those who contradict him."

Paul instructs Titus to hold fast to the faithful word and to have power both to exhort by right teaching and to convict those who contradict the truth.

Sound, disciplined teaching is a defense against the spread of deceptive practices and distorted doctrines. Church leaders have the responsibility to faithfully teach the Word of God, confronting and correcting any teaching that deviates from the truth revealed in Scripture.

The faithful's responsibility to denounce deceptive practices and protect the community of faith against false prophets is essential for preserving the doctrinal integrity of the Church. Fulfilling this responsibility requires being vigilant, seeking wisdom and discernment, acting with love and truth in confrontation, identifying the signs of false prophets, seeking restoration for those involved in deception, and promoting sound and disciplined teaching.

By acting on the Word of God and the guidance of the Holy Spirit, we strengthen our religious community against the dangers posed by false prophets and authentically and powerfully witness true faith in Christ. May we assume this responsibility with courage, love and humility, aiming to build and protect the church of Christ in the midst of a world full of deceit and falsehood.

FRATERNAL LOVE AND COMMUNION

Brotherly love and fellowship among believers are key to strengthening our defense against the influence of false prophets. In this chapter, we will address the importance of unity within the Christian community, supporting each other in our search for truth and discernment.

The Importance of Brotherly Love

Brotherly love is one of the pillars of Jesus Christ's teaching and is essential for identifying and rejecting false prophets. This kind of love is characterized by altruism, kindness, and genuine concern for the well-being of other members of the faith community.

John 13:34-35 "A new commandment I give to you, that you love one another; as I have loved you, that you also love one another. By this all will know that you are my disciples, if you have love for one another."

In this passage, Jesus makes it clear that mutual love is a hallmark of His disciples. Through brotherly love, Christians witness to the world the true nature of their faith and reinforce unity within the community of believers.

The Exhortation to Unity in the Church

The Bible often emphasizes the importance of unity within the church as it is a defense against the influence of false prophets.

1 Corinthians 1:10 "I beseech you, brethren, by the name of our Lord Jesus Christ, that you all speak the same thing and that there be no divisions among you, but that you be completely united, in the same mental disposition and in the same opinion."

Paul exhorts the Corinthians not to have divisions among themselves, but to be entirely united in the same mind and judgment. Unity in the church is an expression of brotherly love and a defense against false teachings and divisions that can weaken the community of faith.

Communion as a Practice of Integration

Communion among the faithful is an essential practice to strengthen fraternal ties and unity within the Christian community.

Acts 2:42 "And they continued steadfastly in the apostles' doctrine and fellowship, in the breaking of bread and in prayers."

The book of Acts describes the practice of fellowship among early Christians. They persevered in the apostles' doctrine and fellowship, demonstrating a life of mutual sharing and fellowship in the faith.

Fellowship involves the sharing of experiences, prayers, needs, and blessings among members of the faith community. This practice strengthens unity and provides an environment conducive to discerning the truth and protecting against false prophets.

Caring for the Weak in Faith

Brotherly love also involves caring for brothers who are weaker in the faith, who may be more susceptible to the influence of false prophets.

Romans 14:1 "Now welcome those who are weak in the faith, but not to discuss opinions."

Paul exhorts Christians to welcome those who are weak in the faith, but not to discuss opinions. Caring for those weak in faith involves patience, understanding, and a willingness to teach them in a loving, truthful way from God's Word.

By taking care of each other, especially the most vulnerable brothers, we strengthen our community of faith and make it harder for false prophets to work.

The Example of the Bereans in Discerning the Truth

The Bereans are an outstanding example of how brotherly love and the pursuit of truth can coexist, resulting in a faith grounded in discernment.

Acts 17:11 "And these were more noble than those in Thessalonica, in that they received the word with all eagerness, examining the Scriptures daily to see whether these things were so."

The Bereans were commended for their nobility, for they gladly received the word preached by Paul and Silas, but not before examining the Scriptures daily to see if what they had been taught was indeed true.

This example shows how the search for the truth can be allied to brotherly love, ensuring that faith is established on a solid foundation and protected against falsehoods.

Mutual Support in Faith

Communion among believers also provides mutual support in the search for truth and discernment. When we are united in love and commitment to the Word of God, we are strengthened and encouraged to persevere in genuine faith.

Hebrews 10:24-25 "And let us consider one another to spur one another on to love and good works, not forsaking the congregation of ourselves, as some have the habit of admonishing, and so much the more as you see the Day approaching."

The author of Hebrews encourages believers to consider one another, encouraging love and good works. Fellowship and mutual encouragement are essential to strengthen the faith community and to protect it from the negative influences of false prophets.

The Admonition in Love

Mutual admonition within the faith community is an act of love and care that contributes to spiritual growth and discernment of truth.

Colossians 3:16 "Let the word of Christ dwell in you richly; instruct and advise one another in all wisdom, praising God in psalms and hymns and spiritual songs with thankfulness in your hearts."

Paul instructs the Colossians to dwell the word of Christ richly in their lives, instructing and advising one another in all wisdom.

Loving admonition is a necessary practice to correct, edify, and protect the community of faith against doctrinal deviations and misleading practices.

Trust in Apostolic Teaching

Unity and brotherly love are also related to confidence in apostolic teaching, which is a safeguard against falsehoods.

2 Thessalonians 2:15 "Therefore, brethren, stand firm and hold the traditions which you were taught, whether by word or by our epistle."

Paul encourages the Thessalonians to stand firm and hold fast to the traditions which they were taught by the apostles, whether by word or epistle.

This reliance on apostolic teaching is a defense against distorted and misleading teaching, as it points us back to the original source of truth and guides us toward genuine faith.

The Role of Leaders in the Community

Leaders within the faith community have a key role in strengthening unity and brotherly love.

1 Pedro 5:2-3 "Shepherd the flock of God which is among you, not under compulsion, but willingly, as God would have it; not for filthy lucre, but willingly; neither as lording it over those entrusted to you, but becoming examples of the flock."

Peter instructs leaders to shepherd the flock of God with genuine and loving motives, being role models for other believers. Leaders have a responsibility to guide the faith community based on the truth of God's Word, protecting it from false teachings and deceptive practices.

The Fruit of the Spirit and the Defense Against Lying

The fruit of the Holy Spirit is a practical expression of brotherly love and unity within the Christian community.

Galatians 5:22-23 "But the fruit of the Spirit is love, joy, peace, longsuffering, gentleness, goodness, faithfulness, gentleness, self-control. Against these things there is no law."

The fruit of the Spirit includes love, kindness, faithfulness, and meekness, essential characteristics for resisting the divisions and conflicts that can be caused by the influence of false prophets.

Brotherly love and fellowship are essential to strengthen the defense against the influence of false prophets. Unity within the Christian community, care for the weak in the faith, admonition in love, trust in apostolic teaching, and the fruit of the Spirit are powerful tools to protect our faith community against deceptive practices and false teachings.

As we love one another, seek the truth together, and support one another in the pursuit of genuine faith, we witness to the world the authenticity of the gospel of Christ and strengthen our ability to resist the negative influences of false prophets. May we, in love and unity, stand firm in the truth of God and defend the purity of faith in Christ within the community of believers.

MERCY AND FORGIVENESS

Even in the face of errors and sins, mercy and forgiveness are essential pillars of the Catholic faith. In this chapter, we will reflect on how to meet the challenges posed by false prophets with compassion and a willingness to reconcile.

Divine Mercy and Our Responsibility

Mercy is a fundamental characteristic of God's character, and as His followers, we are called to emulate this virtue in our lives and relationships.

Ephesians 2:4-5 "But God, being rich in mercy, because of the great love wherewith he loved us, even when we were dead in our trespasses, made us alive together with Christ, - by grace are ye saved."

Paul points out that God is rich in mercy and loved us with a great love, even when we were in our sins. This divine mercy is the source of our salvation and calls us to show compassion and forgiveness to others, regardless of their faults and mistakes.

Forgiveness and Reconciliation

Forgiveness is a central theme in the teaching of Jesus Christ, who exhorts us to forgive as we have been forgiven by God.

Matthew 6:14-15 "For if you forgive men their trespasses, your heavenly Father will also forgive you; but if you do not forgive men [their trespasses], neither will your Father forgive your trespasses."

Jesus makes it clear that forgiveness is an essential attitude in the life of the Christian. If we forgive others, we will be forgiven by God. This connection between human forgiveness and divine forgiveness emphasizes the importance of mutual forgiveness in the faith community.

Forgiveness is also closely linked to reconciliation. By forgiving, we open the way for reconciliation with those who may have been influenced by false prophets and strayed from the true faith. Compassion and a willingness to forgive are key to bringing back those who have strayed from the path of truth.

The Example of Jesus Christ

The example of Jesus Christ is the greatest demonstration of mercy and forgiveness. Even in the face of betrayal, denial, and rejection, He manifested compassion and offered forgiveness to those who had wronged Him.

Lucas 23:34 "Father, forgive them, for they don't know what they are doing."

At the time of His crucifixion, Jesus prayed to the Father, asking forgiveness for those who were crucifying Him. This act of forgiveness is a powerful testimony of God's love and mercy, even to those who persecuted Him.

Jesus also taught about the need to repeatedly forgive our brothers, emphasizing that there are no limits to the compassion and mercy we should extend to others.

Matthew 18:21-22 " Then Peter, approaching, asked him: Lord, how many times will my brother sin against me, that I forgive him? Up to seven times?

Jesus' teaching invites us to forgive unconditionally and extend a hand of reconciliation, even when we are repeatedly hurt.

Forgiveness and Healing Wounds

Forgiveness not only enables us to face the challenges posed by false prophets, it also leads us to heal the emotional and spiritual wounds caused by disappointments and betrayals.

Colossians 3:13 "Bear with one another, forgive each other if anyone has a grievance against another. As the Lord forgave you, so also you must forgive."

Paul exhorts the Colossians to bear with one another and to forgive one another, just as the Lord forgave them. Forgiveness is a therapeutic action that frees the heart from the bonds of grudge and resentment.

When we face the disappointments caused by false prophets with compassion and forgiveness, we not only protect our faith, but we also promote inner healing, allowing God's love and peace to flow into our lives.

Mercy and Judgment

Mercy and forgiveness do not imply ignoring the importance of discernment and fair judgment within the faith community.

John 7:24 "Do not judge according to appearance, but judge according to right justice."

Jesus instructs his disciples to judge with righteous justice, not just based on appearance or the superficiality of situations.

Discernment is essential to identify false prophets and their deceptive practices. We must carefully evaluate the teachings and revelations that arise within the community of faith, against the Word of God, before making any decision or pronouncing any judgment.

Admonition with Mercy

Admonition is an important practice in the faith community, but it must be done with compassion and mercy.

Galatians 6:1 "Brothers, if a man is caught in any trespass, you who are spiritual restore such a one in a spirit of gentleness; and take heed to yourself, lest you also be tempted."

Paul exhorts the brethren to forward those who have been caught in some offense in a spirit of gentleness. Admonition must be guided by love and a desire for restoration rather than condemnation and harsh judgment.

Merciful admonition allows false prophets the opportunity to repent and return to the true faith, while protecting the faith community from deception and harmful practices.

Mercy and the Call to Conversion

Mercy is a call to conversion and repentance.

Lucas 5:31-32 "But Jesus answered them, The healthy do not need a doctor, but the sick; I did not come to call the righteous, but sinners to repentance."

Jesus made it clear that He came to call sinners to repentance. Divine mercy is always open to repentant hearts, willing to forsake sin and follow the truth.

God's love invites us to abandon our wrong ways and turn to Him, seeking forgiveness and reconciliation. Likewise, the mercy we show others should always point to repentance and a return to genuine faith in Christ.

Forgiveness as a Source of Freedom

Forgiveness is a source of freedom, both for the forgiver and for the forgiven.

Matthew 18:23-27 "For this reason the kingdom of heaven is like a king who decided to settle accounts with his servants. And when he went to do so, they brought him one who owed him ten thousand talents. But when he had nothing to pay, his lord ordered that he, his wife, and children, and all that he owned, be sold, so that the debt might be paid. and forgave him the debt."

In this parable told by Jesus, the king forgives the great debt of the servant who owed him ten thousand talents. This forgiveness results in freedom for the servant, who was about to be sold into slavery to pay his debt.

Likewise, the forgiveness we extend to others frees us from the prison of hatred, resentment and the desire for revenge. Forgiveness enables us to move forward with a light heart and free from emotional ties.

The Role of the Community in Reconciliation

The faith community plays a vital role in seeking reconciliation among members who may have been affected by the influences of false prophets.

Matthew 18:15 "If your brother sins [against you], go reason with him between you and him alone. If he listens to you, you have gained your brother."

Jesus instructs His disciples to go directly to the brother who has sinned against them, privately seeking reconciliation. This process of loving and merciful confrontation can pave the way for relationship restoration and a return to true faith.

The faith community must be willing to intervene with compassion and guidance, facilitating dialogue and encouraging reconciliation among those who may have been affected by the influences of false prophets.

Hope in Divine Forgiveness

Hope in divine forgiveness is a source of consolation and strength for the community of faith.

1 John 1:9 "If we confess our sins, he is faithful and just to forgive us our sins and to cleanse us from all unrighteousness."

John assures us that if we confess our sins, God is faithful and just to forgive us and to cleanse us from all unrighteousness. This promise is a source of hope for those who have strayed from the path and seek restoration in God's mercy.

Mercy and forgiveness are essential pillars of the Catholic faith, founded on the example of Jesus Christ and the loving character of God. As we face the challenges posed by false prophets, we must act with compassion and a willingness to reconcile, following Christ's example and seeking healing from the wounds caused by disappointments and betrayals.

Forgiveness is a powerful tool for restoring relationships and protecting the faith community against doctrinal deviations. Divine mercy calls us to repentance and conversion, and also inspires us to extend the hand of reconciliation to those who have strayed from the path of truth.

May we be bearers of mercy and forgiveness, demonstrating God's love in our actions and words, and protecting our community of faith against the challenges posed by false prophets, with the certainty that hope in divine forgiveness is an inexhaustible source of consolation and strengthening.

HOPE IN TRUTH

Concluding our journey, we will reaffirm the hope we have in the true word of God and the protection He gives us against false prophets. In this chapter, we will find inspiration to move forward, strengthened in our faith and confident in divine wisdom.

77

The Promise of Preservation of Truth

God promises to preserve His word and protect His faithful against the onslaught of false prophets.

Isaiah 40:8 "The grass withers, the flower fades, but the word of our God stands forever."

This passage from Isaiah emphasizes the eternity of God's word. While the grass withers and the flower falls, divine truth remains unshakable. Hope is actually based on the certainty that God's Word is unchanging and reliable, guiding us along our journey of faith.

Trust in the Word of God

The Psalms invite us to trust God's Word as a source of refuge and protection.

Salmo 119:105 "Your word is a lamp to my feet, a light to my path."

Psalm 119 underscores the importance of the Word of God in our lives. She is like a lamp that illuminates our steps and a light that guides us in the midst of darkness. Relying on God's Word enables us to discern truth and guard against false teachings.

The Wisdom That Comes From God

Divine wisdom is an antidote against the influence of false prophets. As we seek the wisdom that comes from God, we will be strengthened to discern the truth.

Proverbs 2:6 "For the Lord gives wisdom, and understanding and understanding come from his mouth."

Wisdom is not the fruit of human knowledge, but a gift from God. As we seek divine wisdom, we are guided to understand the truth and avoid the pitfalls of deception.

The Protection of the Good Shepherd

Jesus is the Good Shepherd who protects His sheep from false prophets and spiritual dangers.

John 10:11 "I am the good shepherd; the good shepherd lays down his life for the sheep."

In this passage, Jesus presents himself as the Good Shepherd who is willing to lay down His life for the sheep. His love and care are unconditional, protecting us from spiritual threats and attacks from false prophets.

The Holy Spirit as Guide

The Holy Ghost is our guide and counselor, enabling us to discern truth and follow God's way.

John 16:13 "When the Spirit of truth comes, he will guide you into all the truth; for he will not speak on his own, but whatever he hears he will speak, and he will declare to you the things to come."

Jesus promised that when the Spirit of truth comes, He will guide us into all truth. The Holy Spirit enables us to understand the Word of God and to discern between truth and lies, protecting us against the deceptions of false prophets.

The Victory in Christ

In Christ, we have victory over deceit and falsehood.

1 Corinthians 15:57 "Thanks be to God, who gives us the victory through our Lord Jesus Christ."

Paul extols God for giving us the victory through Jesus Christ. This victory includes protection against the onslaught of false prophets and the confidence that, in Christ, we are more than conquerors.

The Armor of God

Ephesians 6:10-11 "Finally, be strong in the Lord and in the power of his might. Put on the whole armor of God, that you may be able to stand against the wiles of the devil."

The armor of God is a powerful metaphor that reminds us of the importance of putting on the power of God to face the attacks of false prophets. This armor includes the belt of truth, the breastplate of righteousness, the preparation of the gospel of peace, the shield of faith, the helmet of salvation, and the sword of the Spirit, which is the Word of God.

The armor of God protects us against the wiles of the devil and strengthens us to stand firm in the truth and in genuine faith.

The Fight for the Faith

The apostle Paul uses combat language to describe the struggle for genuine faith.

1 Timothy 6:12 "Fight the good fight of faith; win eternal life, to which you were also called and of which you made the good confession in the presence of many witnesses."

Paul exhorts Timothy to fight the good fight of faith, resisting false teachings and protecting the truth entrusted to him. This struggle for faith is an expression of our hope in God's truth and protection.

The Quest for Knowledge

The quest for knowledge of the Word of God is fundamental to strengthen our faith and discern the truth.

Hosea 4:6 "My people are being destroyed for lack of knowledge."

The prophet Hosea warns about the destruction caused by lack of knowledge. Knowing God's Word enables us to identify false teachings and protect our faith against the negative influences of false prophets.

Hope in the Coming of Christ

Our ultimate hope is in the coming of Christ, who will bring the fullness of truth and righteousness.

Tito 2:13 "looking for the blessed hope and glorious appearing of our great God and Savior Jesus Christ."

Paul encourages believers to look forward to the blessed hope of Christ's coming. This hope inspires us to persevere in genuine faith and to remain vigilant against the deceptions of false prophets.

REVELATIONS OF THE ANCIENT

The teachings contained in Deuteronomy echoed through the centuries, warning about the dangers of being influenced by false thoughts and prophesying what does not come from God. Ancient warnings came to life in the present day, where many preachers correctly shared the divine word, but their minds became vulnerable to deceitful voices.

Deuteronomy 18:9-13 - The Prohibition of Divination

In the book of Deuteronomy, we find an emphatic warning against the practice of divination and other forms of witchcraft and occultism:

"When you come into the land which the LORD your God gives you, you shall not learn to do after the abominations of those nations. There shall not be found among you anyone who makes his son or his daughter pass through the fire, or one who uses divination, or a soothsayer, or an omen, or a sorcerer, or an enchanter, or one who consults a spirit of divination, or a sorcerer, or one who consults the dead; for everyone who does such a thing is an abomination to the LORD; and for these abominations the LORD your God drives them out. before you. You shall be perfect with the Lord your God." (Deuteronomy 18:9-13)

In this passage, God instructs His people to turn away from the pagan practices of the surrounding nations. It explicitly forbids divination, the use of divine spirits, sorcery, and any form of consulting the dead. The reason behind this prohibition is clear: such practices are abominations before the Lord, and those who engage in them are separated from God's presence.

That warning remains relevant today as we too face temptations to seek knowledge and guidance outside of God's Word. Divination and other forms of occultism are a trap that can lead believers to deviate from the true faith, falling into the trap of false prophets.

Jeremiah 14:14-16 - The Condemnation of the Deceiving Prophets

Jeremiah, one of the Old Testament prophets, had the challenge of facing false prophets who spread lies and deceit among the people of Israel:

"Then the Lord said to me, The prophets prophesy lies in my name; I did not send them, nor commanded them, nor spoke to them; false vision, soothsaying, vanity, and the deceitfulness of their heart are what they prophesy to you. Therefore, thus said the Lord concerning the prophets who prophesy in my name, although I sent them, but who say, Sword and famine shall not be in this land: by sword and famine shall those prophets be consumed. And the people whom they prophesy shall be cast into the lands. streets of Jerusalem, because of the famine and the sword; and there will be none to bury them, nor their wives, nor their children; and I will pour out their own iniquity upon them." (Jeremiah 14:14-16)

In this passage, Jeremiah denounces the false prophets who prophesied lies in the name of the Lord. They were deceiving the people with false promises of prosperity and security when, in fact, the nation was about to face divine judgment.

These deceitful prophets are condemned by God, and the consequence of their lies would be the famine and the sword that would devastate the people of Israel. This serves as a warning to all who are called to preach the Word of God: we must be careful not to distort or tamper with the divine message, for the responsibility of guiding the souls of the faithful is a serious and sacred task.

Ezekiel 13:1-10 - The Warning to False Prophets

The prophet Ezekiel was also inspired to confront the false prophets of his day:

"The word of the LORD came to me, saying, Son of man, prophesy against the prophets of Israel who prophesy, and say to the prophets that come out of their own hearts, Hear the word of the LORD. falsehood; they that do so speak a vision out of their own heart, and not from the mouth of the LORD. Say unto them that have preached a false vision, It shall not come to pass, neither shall it be done: for it is in their hearts that they prophesy vanity. Thus saith the Lord GOD; Because ye speak vanity, and see a lie, therefore, behold, I am against you, saith the Lord GOD. in the rolls of the house of Israel and the land of Israel they shall not come; and you will know that I am the Lord God."(Ezekiel 13:1-10)

Ezekiel receives a message from God to prophesy against the prophets of Israel who followed their own hearts and not the voice of the Lord. These false prophets were uttering false visions and deceitful divinations, spreading lies among the people.

The Lord declares that He is against these deceiving prophets and that they will have no place in the council of His people, nor will they be written in the rolls of the house of Israel. This passage highlights the seriousness of the responsibility of those who call themselves prophets or preachers of the Word of God. We must be diligent in listening to the voice of the Lord and not speak visions and prophecies that come from our own hearts, but rather be faithful in transmitting the truth that comes from the Most High.

Zechariah 13:3 - The End of False Prophets

Zechariah, another Old Testament prophet, speaks of a time when false prophets will no longer influence God's people:

"And it shall come to pass, when any man yet prophesy, his father and his mother, which begat him, shall say unto him, Thou shalt not live, because thou speakest a lie in the name of the Lord; and his father and mother, which begat him, shall pierce him through when he prophesy."(Zechariah 13:3)

This passage describes a situation where the deceitful prophets would be rejected even by their own fathers, as the people would recognize the falsehood of their words. This rejection of false prophets is a demonstration of the faithfulness and discernment of God's people regarding the true Word of the Lord.

In this vision, the prophet is pointing to the time when lies and deceit will be dispelled, and only the truth will prevail. It reminds us that even amidst the deceptions caused by false prophets, God is faithful to reveal truth and protect His faithful ones.

Micah 3:5-7 - The Prophets Who Speak for Evil

The prophet Micah also addresses the issue of false prophets who distort God's message:

"Thus saith the Lord concerning the prophets which lead my people astray, which, biting with their teeth, cry, Peace; but against him that puteth nothing in their mouth they prepare war.

Therefore the night shall be dark for you, without vision, and the darkness without divination; and the sun shall go down upon the prophets, and the day shall be black upon them. there will be no answer from God." (Micah 3:5-7)

In this text, Miqueias denounces the prophets who distort God's message, making the people err and crying out for peace when war was about to happen. They sought personal benefit and did not care about truth and justice.

Micah prophesies that darkness and blindness would fall upon these deceiving prophets, and God's answer would be withheld from them. This passage reinforces the idea that God does not reveal himself to those who manipulate His Word to suit their own interests, and that divine judgment will fall on those who deceive the people in the name of the Lord.

THE PATH OF TWISTED TRUTHS

In this chapter, we will enter the labyrinth of the human mind, where the quest to understand and interpret divine revelations can lead to dangerous deviations. Preachers, desirous of being instruments of the Most High, are faced with the dilemma of discerning between authentic voices and the seductive whispers of false deities.

2 Peter 3:15-16 - The Warning About Distorting the Scriptures

Peter, one of the apostles of Jesus Christ, wrote a letter in which he warned about the tendency of some people to distort the Scriptures to suit their own interests:

"And reckon the longsuffering of our Lord to be salvation; as our beloved brother Paul also wrote to you, according to the wisdom given him; speaking of this, as in all his epistles, among which are points hard to be understood, which the unlearned and unstable wrest, and likewise the other Scriptures, to their own destruction." (2 Pedro 3:15-16)

In this passage, Peter highlights the wisdom present in Paul's writings, but also warns that some misinterpret and distort his words, as well as other Scriptures, to suit their own desires and interests.

This warning remains relevant today, where the interpretation of Scripture can be influenced by many factors, such as prejudices, personal ambitions and doctrinal deviations. Preachers and religious leaders must be careful to avoid twisting divine truths in order to ensure that the message conveyed is in line with God's purpose.

Matthew 7:15-20 - False Prophets Recognized by Their Fruit

Jesus warned His disciples about false prophets, revealing that we would recognize them by the fruit they bear:

"Beware of false prophets, which come to you in sheep's clothing, but inwardly they are ravening wolves. By their fruit you will know them. Are grapes gathered from thornbushes or figs from thistles? So every good tree bears good fruit, but a bad tree bears bad fruit. A good tree cannot bear bad fruit, nor can a bad tree produce good fruit. Every tree that does not produce good fruit is cut down and thrown into the fire. Therefore, by their fruits you will know them."(Matthew 7:15-20)

Jesus emphasizes the importance of discerning between true and false prophets. False prophets may appear harmless and even godly on the outside, but their intentions and teachings are deceitful and harmful.

The metaphor of trees and their fruit highlights the connection between a person's essence and their actions. Just as a good tree bears good fruit, a true prophet of God will bring teachings and results that are uplifting and in line with divine principles. On the other hand, a false prophet will produce evil fruit, the consequences of which are harmful to the flock of God.

This passage reminds us of the importance of carefully examining the teachings of those who claim to be spiritual leaders in order to avoid being misled by false doctrines.

1 John 4:1 - The Testing of the Spirits

The apostle John also exhorts us to test the spirits to discern truth from falsehood:

"Beloved, believe not every spirit, but try the spirits whether they are of God: because many false prophets are gone out into the world." (1 John 4:1)

In this passage, John warns believers not to believe any spirit or teaching they encounter, but to test it to see if it is from God. He warns that many false prophets are in the world, ready to spread deception and deviations from the true message of God.

The testing of the spirits involves evaluating statements and teachings in light of the Word of God and the character of Christ. If doctrines and prophecies do not conform to the truth revealed in the Scriptures, they must be rejected as false.

This teaching is fundamental for religious leaders and preachers, as it helps them to discern between what comes from the Spirit of God and what is a mere illusion or human creation. Only by being guided by the Holy Spirit and grounded in the

Word of God can they avoid falling into the traps of false teachings.

Galatians 1:6-9 - The Warning Against the False Gospel

Paul, in his letter to the Galatians, expresses his concern about the rapid change of some believers to a false gospel:

"I am astonished that you are so soon deserting Him who called you in the grace of Christ, to another gospel; which is no other, except that there are some who disturb you and want to pervert the gospel of Christ. But even if we ourselves or an angel from heaven should preach to you any other gospel than what we have preached to you, let him be accursed.(Galatians 1:6-9)

Paul is amazed at how quickly the Galatians are deserting the true gospel of Christ and turning to a distorted version. He warns them that any teaching other than what they initially received is a false gospel and must be rejected.

This passage reinforces the importance of standing firm in the truth and genuine doctrine of Christ. Preachers and religious leaders must be vigilant in maintaining the integrity of divine truths and avoiding any form of twisting or tampering with Scripture.

Acts 20:28-31 - The Protection of the Flock of God

In his address to the Ephesian elders, Paul warns them about false prophets and their mission to protect the flock of God:

"Take heed therefore to yourselves, and to all the flock, over which the Holy Ghost hath made you overseers, to shepherd the church of God, which he purchased with his own blood. For I know this, that after my departure shall savage wolves enter in among you, not sparing the flock. And that of your own selves shall men arise, speaking perverse things, to draw away disciples after them. , I did not cease to admonish each one with tears."(Acts 20:28-31)

Paul emphasizes the responsibility of church leaders to protect the flock of God from false teachings and prophets. He warns them that, after his departure, cruel wolves will appear who will not hesitate to devour the flock. Furthermore, there will be men who will arise from within the Christian community itself, propagating evil teachings to attract followers to themselves.

Paul exhorts leaders to watch and be vigilant regarding doctrine, remembering their duty to admonish the people with love and dedication. This passage reinforces the importance of spiritual leadership in protecting God's flock from the dangers of false doctrines and prophets.

95

THE SEDUCTION OF FALSE PROPHETS

The voices of false prophets are like catchy melodies, which numb the hearers and lead them away from the true light. In this chapter, we'll explore how misleading promises can lead believers to worship false gods without realizing it, compromising their genuine faith.

Jeremiah 23:16-17 - Prophets Announcing Deceit

Jeremiah, once again, denounces false prophets who spread deceit among God's people:

"Thus saith the Lord of hosts, Hear not the words of the prophets which prophesy among you; they make you faint; they speak from the vision of their own heart, not from the mouth of the Lord. (Jeremiah 23:16-17)

In this passage, God warns His people not to listen to false prophets who proclaim visions and revelations that come from their own hearts and not from the mouth of the Lord. These deceitful prophets make people fade away, that is, they lead them into deception and illusion.

They speak of peace and prosperity for those who despise the Word of the Lord and follow their own desires and purposes. In doing so, these false prophets seduce listeners with tempting promises, leading them away from the true faith and the way of God.

This warning is valid today, where we also face the temptation to follow teachings that appeal to our selfish desires and distance us from God's will. We must be careful to discern between the authentic voices that emanate from the Word of God and the illusory messages that come from human hearts.

Jesus also warned of the coming of false Christs and false prophets in the last days:

"For false Christs and false prophets will arise, performing great signs and wonders to deceive, if possible, the very elect." (Matthew 24:24)

In this passage, Jesus makes a prediction about the end times, warning that false Christs and false prophets will arise and perform great signs and wonders to deceive people, including God's elect.

This prophecy is a reminder that not all signs and wonders are authentic and from God. False prophets can perform impressive feats, but their goal is to divert people from true faith in Christ and lead them to worship false deities.

It is essential for believers to be rooted in the Word of God and have spiritual discernment so as not to be deceived by the deceptive appearances of false prophets. Confidence in the truth of Christ and His Word is the best defense against the temptations and seductions of false teaching.

1 Timothy 4:1-3 - False Teachings and Seared Consciences

Paul warns Timothy of false teachings that would spread in later times:

"But the Spirit expressly says that in later times some will fall away from the faith, giving heed to deceitful spirits and doctrines of demons, through the hypocrisy of men who speak lies and have seared their own consciences, who forbid marriage and enjoin abstinence from foods which God created to be received with thanksgiving by those who believe and by those who fully know the truth."(1 Timothy 4:1-3)

In this passage, Paul emphasizes that, in later times, some will fall away from genuine faith by listening to deceitful spirits and doctrines of demons. False prophets, driven by hypocrisy and lies, lead people into error and apostasy.

Furthermore, these false teachings can result in the searing of conscience, that is, people can lose moral sensitivity and the ability to discern right from wrong.

Paul specifically mentions those who forbid marriage and command abstinence from foods that God created to be received with thanksgiving. This is a reference to teachings that promote extreme asceticism and deny God's creation as good.

This passage warns us about the seduction of false teachings that can lead people to abandon the true faith and compromise their conscience and discernment. We must be aware and grounded in biblical truth to avoid falling into the traps of misleading doctrines.

2 Corinthians 11:13-15 - The False Apostles

Paul also discusses the threat posed by false apostles who masquerade as servants of Christ:

"For such men are false apostles, deceitful workers, disguising themselves as the apostles of Christ.(2 Corinthians 11:13-15)

In this passage, Paul denounces false apostles who present themselves as servants of Christ, but in reality are deceitful workers. Just as Satan disguises himself as an angel of light, these false prophets also disguise themselves to deceive God's people.

These false apostles may appear convincing and righteous, but their true intent is to further their own agendas and lead people astray from the true faith in Christ.

This passage is a powerful warning about the seduction of false prophets who seek to confuse and divert the faithful from the true path of faith. It reminds us that although they may appear to be genuine and godly, their true nature will be revealed by their works and fruit.

Revelation 13:11-15 - The False Prophet

In the book of Revelation, a vision of the false prophet is presented, who works together with the antichrist, deceiving people with miracles and wonders:

"And I saw another beast rise out of the earth. It had two horns like a lamb, but it spoke like a dragon. It exercised all the authority of the first beast before it. It made the earth and its inhabitants worship the first beast, whose deadly wound had been healed. And it performed great signs, even causing fire to come down from heaven to the earth in the sight of men. And by the miracles that it was permitted to perform in the name of the first beast, it deceived the inhabitants of the earth. to the beast that was wounded by the sword and yet lived. And it was given to him to give breath to the image of the first beast, so that the image could speak and order to kill all who did not worship it."(Revelation 13:11-15)

In this passage, the performance of the false prophet who deceives the inhabitants of the earth through signs and miracles is described. He exercises authority and influence, leading people to worship the first beast, which is a figure associated with the Antichrist.

This apocalyptic vision alerts us to the seductive influence of false prophets in the last days, who will use signs and wonders to deceive and lead people away from true faith in God.

THE THIN LINE OF DEVOTION

The worship of false gods can begin subtly, as the desire to receive divine revelations mixes with impatience to wait for God's timing. We will see how this fine line between genuine devotion and idolatry can be inadvertently crossed, dragging well-meaning hearts into the abyss of falsehood.

Exodus 32:1-8 - The Worship of the Golden Calf

One of the most emblematic passages that illustrate the fine line between devotion and idolatry is the story of the golden calf, recorded in the book of Exodus:

"Now when the people saw that Moses delayed going down the mountain, they came to Aaron and said to him, Arise, make us gods that go before us; for as for this Moses, the man who brought us up out of the land of Egypt, we do not know what has become of him. their ears, and brought them to Aaron. He took them from their hand, cast them into a mold, and made them into a molten calf. Then they said, "Behold, O Israel, your god, who brought you out of the land of Egypt." When Aaron saw it, he built an altar before the calf, and proclaimed, and said, "Tomorrow there will be a feast to the LORD. The next day they rose early, and offered burnt offerings, and brought peace offerings; and the people sat down to eat and drink; , got up to play."(Exodus 32:1-6)

In this passage, after Moses went up Mount Sinai to receive the Law of God, the people of Israel, impatient and insecure, asked Aaron to make gods for them. Aaron gives in to pressure and casts a golden calf to be worshiped by the people as a symbol of divinity.

104

Although the initial objective was to have a representative figure of God, the people's action was a deviation from true devotion and faith in Yahweh, the God of Israel. They sought a quick, tangible solution to their need for spiritual leadership rather than patiently trusting God's providence and plan.

This passage reminds us of the temptation to look for shortcuts to fellowship with God. Impatience and the search for immediate revelations can lead to the worship of idols and false gods. We must learn to wait patiently for God's timing, trusting in His wisdom and care for us.

2 Kings 18:1-4 - The End of the Brazen Serpent

The book of 2 Kings relates the episode of the bronze serpent, which was initially a divine institution to heal the people of Israel, but ended up becoming an object of idolatry:

"In the third year of Hoshea son of Elah king of Israel began Hezekiah son of Ahaz king of Judah to reign. He was twenty-five years old when he began to reign, and he reigned twenty-nine years in Jerusalem; his mother was named Abi, daughter of Zechariah. bronze serpent that Moses had made, because until that day the children of Israel burned incense to it and called it Neustan." (2 Kings 18:1-4)

This passage relates the religious reform undertaken by King Hezekiah in Judah. Although he was a just and righteous king in the eyes of God, he realized that the bronze serpent, made by Moses in the desert under divine guidance to heal the people from the bites of poisonous serpents (Numbers 21:4-9), had become an object of idolatrous worship.

Originally, the bronze serpent served as a symbol of divine healing and deliverance, representing God's mercy and salvation. However, over time, the people began to burn incense to her and call her "Neustan", making her an idol.

King Hezekiah recognized the seriousness of this practice and destroyed the bronze serpent to eliminate idolatry. This action shows the importance of preserving pure devotion to God and not allowing even sacred symbols and objects to become sources of idolatry.

This story teaches us that the fine line between genuine devotion and idolatry can be easily crossed when we lose sight of the original meaning of sacred symbols and objects and turn them into objects of worship.

2 Corinthians 11:2-4 - The Danger of Seduction

Paul expresses his concern for the Corinthian church, fearing that they might be seduced by misleading teachings and turn away from pure devotion to Christ:

"For I am jealous for you with a godly jealousy; for I have prepared you to present you as a chaste virgin to one husband, even to Christ. But I am afraid, lest, as the serpent deceived Eve in his cunning, so also your senses might be corrupted, and depart from the simplicity and purity that is in Christ. behold." (2 Corinthians 11:2-4)

In this passage, Paul compares the Corinthian church to a chaste virgin who must be presented to Christ. He expresses his concern that the church could be seduced and corrupted by false teachings, just as Eve was deceived by the serpent in the Garden of Eden.

Paul fears that the Corinthians might drift away from the simplicity and purity of devotion to Christ, embracing another Jesus, another spirit, or another gospel other than the true one taught by him and the apostles.

This passage highlights the danger of seduction and false doctrine that can lead well-meaning hearts away from true faith in Christ. We must be watchful and vigilant against deceptive teachings that might divert our devotion from the true God.

Colossians 2:8-10 - Beware of Human Traditions

Paul exhorts the Colossians to beware of human traditions and vain teachings that can distract from genuine devotion to Christ:

"Take care lest anyone ensnare you with his philosophy and vain deceit, after the tradition of men, after the rudiments of the world, and not after Christ: for in him all the fullness of the Godhead dwelleth bodily. And ye are complete in him, who is the head of all principality and power." (Colossians 2:8-10)

In this passage, Paul warns against the influence of human philosophies and vain traditions that are not rooted in Christ. He emphasizes that the fullness of the Godhead dwells in Christ and that therefore we should center our devotion on Him.

This passage warns us not to be ensnared by human ideas and traditions that can divert our devotion and faith in the true God. We must stand firm in Christ, acknowledging him as the head of all principality and power, and not allow empty philosophies and teachings to lead us astray from the path of truth.

1 John 5:21 - Beware of idols

The apostle John closes his first epistle with an emphatic warning to guard against idols:

108

"Little children, keep yourselves from idols. Amen!" (1 John 5:21)

This brief but powerful exhortation reminds us of the importance of being on our guard against any form of idolatry or the worship of false gods.

Idols can take on many forms besides statues or physical objects. They can be represented by selfish desires, material ambitions, pursuit of power, or anything that takes precedence over devotion and love for God.

The fine line between genuine devotion and idolatry is often crossed without us realizing it, and it is essential that we are vigilant and grounded in God's Word lest we be dragged into the abyss of falsehood.

TWO SNAPLES LEFT

In this chapter, we will witness stories of dedicated preachers who succumbed to the seduction of false gods. Their mistakes were not the fruit of bad intentions, but the burning desire to be renowned prophets. However, we will learn that even the most sincere souls can get lost in the labyrinths of the mind.

110

The story of Balaam, a prophet mentioned in the Old Testament, is a striking example of someone who was seduced by the desire for personal gain and recognition, leading him to stray from the path of God:

"So Balaam rose up in the morning, saddled his donkey, and went with the princes of Moab. And the anger of God was kindled because he was going away; and the angel of the Lord stood in the way for an adversary to him; he went walking with his two servants, and his donkey was with him. But the donkey saw the angel of the Lord standing in the way, with his drawn sword in his hand; And the angel of the Lord stood in a path among the vineyards, with a wall on one side and on the other. When the donkey saw the angel of the Lord, she leaned against the wall, and pressed Balaam's foot against the wall; so he struck her again. The angel of the Lord lay down under Balaam, and Balaam was enraged and smote the donkey with his staff. Then the Lord opened the donkey's mouth, and she said to Balaam, What have I done to you that you have beaten me these three times? Balaam said to the donkey, Why have you mocked me? I wish I had a sword in my hand, because now I would kill you. The donkey returned to Balaam, Am I not your donkey, on which you have ridden from the time I became yours to this day? Am I in the habit of doing this with you? He replied: No. Then the Lord opened Balaam's eyes, and he saw the angel of the Lord standing in the way, with his drawn sword in his hand; so he bowed his head and prostrated himself with his face to the ground. The Angel of the Lord said to him, Why have you beaten your donkey three times? Behold, I went out to be an adversary on the way, because your conduct is perverse before me."(Numbers 22:21-32)

Balaam was a well-known prophet, and the king of Moab, Balak, summoned him to curse the people of Israel. However, God warned Balaam not to curse the people, for they were blessed by Him.

Although Balaam initially obeyed God, the desire for personal gain led him to try to curse Israel again. God put an Angel in Balaam's way to stop him, but he was so focused on the reward offered by Balac that he didn't realize the danger he faced.

Balaam's story teaches us that even those who have the gift of prophecy can be influenced by the desire for fame, power, and wealth. We must be aware of these temptations and remain faithful to God's purpose in our lives.

Saul, the first king of Israel, was a leader who wanted to please God, but his impatience led him to disobey divine instructions:

"So Saul waited seven days, as Samuel had commanded; but Samuel did not come to Gilgal, and the people were scattered from him. Then Saul said, "Bring me the burnt offering and the peace offerings here." thou didst not come on the appointed days, and the Philistines were assembled at Michmash, I said, Now shall the Philistines come down upon me at Gilgal, and I have not yet implored the favor of the LORD: so I was constrained, and offered up the burnt offering. the Lord gave him a man after his own heart, and the Lord has commanded him to be captain over his people, because you have not kept what the Lord commanded you." (1 Samuel 13:7-14)

In this passage, Saul was about to face the Philistines in battle, and Samuel had instructed Saul to wait seven days before offering a burnt offering to God. However, when the days passed and the people were scattered, Saul gave in to his haste and offered the burnt offering himself, disobeying God's command.

Saul justified his action as a need to seek God's favor before battle, but his impatience led him to disobey and make rash decisions. Because of his disobedience, God withdrew the promise of an enduring kingdom to Saul's lineage, choosing another man, David, to be the king after God's own heart.

This story alerts us to the importance of obeying God's commandments, even when we are facing difficulties or pressures. Impatience and the search for immediate solutions can lead us to make hasty decisions that result in negative consequences.

1 Kings 13:1-34 - The Disobedient Prophet

The story of the unknown prophet, mentioned in 1 Kings 13, is a powerful lesson on obedience to divine instructions:

"And, behold, a man of God came from Judah to Bethel, by the command of the Lord, with Jeroboam standing at the altar to burn incense. And at the command of the Lord he cried against the altar, saying, Altar, altar! Thus saith the Lord, Behold, a son shall be born to the house of David, whose name shall be called Josiah; and the Lord said, Behold, the altar shall be split open, and the ashes that are upon thee shall be poured out." And it came to pass, when the king heard the word of the man of God, who had cried against the altar at Bethel, that Jeroboam stretched out his hand from the altar, saying, Bind him. , according to the sign which the man of God gave by the

114

commandment of the Lord Then the king answered and said to the man of God, Plead favor with the Lord your God, and pray for me, that my hand may be restored to me. The man of God pleaded with the Lord, and the king's hand was restored to him, and it was as before. The king said to the man of God, Come in with me into the house, and I will support you, that you may offer me an offering. But the man of God said to the king, Even if you gave me half of your house, I would not go with you, nor would I eat bread or drink water in this place; for so I was commanded by the word of the Lord, saying: You shall not eat bread, nor drink water, nor go back by the way you came. So he went another way and did not return the way he had come to Bethel. An old prophet dwelt at Bethel; and his sons came and told him all that the man of God had done that day at Bethel; and the words which he had spoken to the king, they also told their father. The father asked them: Which way did he go? For his sons showed him the way that the man of God from Judah had gone. Then he said, "Saddle me on my donkey." And they saddled his donkey, and he mounted it. And he went after the man of God, and found him sitting under an oak; and said to him, Are you the man of God who came from Judah? He answered: I am. Then he said to him, Come home with me and eat bread. He said to him, I will not return with you, nor will I come into your house, nor will I eat bread or drink water with you in this place; for by order of the Lord it was said to me: Thou shalt not eat bread, nor drink water there, nor return by the way whither thou goest. And he said to him, I am a prophet also, like you, and an angel spoke to me by the Lord's command, saying, Bring him back with you to your house, that he may eat bread and drink water. You lied. So he returned by the same way that he had come, and he did not go by the way that the man of God of Judah had told him. Then a lion met him on the way and killed him; and his corpse was lying in the way, and the donkey standing beside him; the lion was also standing beside the corpse. And behold, a man passing by, and seeing the dead body lying on the road and the lion standing by the dead body, went and spoke in the city where the old prophet dwelt. When the prophet who had turned him back by the way heard, he said, This is the man of God, who rebelled against the command of the Lord; So the Lord gave him to the lion, which tore and killed him, according to the word that the Lord had spoken to him." (1 Kings 13:1-34)

In this story, God sent an unknown prophet to pronounce judgment on the altar at Bethel. The prophet fulfilled the mission faithfully, announcing that a descendant of David named Josiah would destroy the idolatrous priests and human bones would be burned on the altar.

King Jeroboam, hearing the prophet's words and seeing the sign of the altar break, stretched out his hand to arrest him, but his hand withered instantly. Afraid and convinced of the prophet's power, the king asked him to intercede for him, and his hand was restored.

So the king invited the prophet to his house to offer him a reward. However, the prophet declined the invitation, remembering God's orders not to eat or drink at Bethel and not to return the same way.

But as the prophet was returning the other way, an elderly prophet, who was also the father of other prophets, heard what had happened at Bethel. He went to the unknown prophet and invited him to his home, claiming that an angel instructed him to bring him back to eat and drink.

Unfortunately, the unknown prophet believed the old prophet's lie and agreed to accompany him home. Returning along this disobedient path, the prophet was killed by a lion, just as God had predicted.

This story is a powerful reminder that we must be careful to discern God's instructions and not get carried away by words that contradict God's Word. Disobedience, even if induced by others who claim to receive divine revelations, can lead to spiritual downfall and serious consequences.

1 Kings 22:1-38 - False Prophets and the Seduction of the Crowd

This story relates an incident where several false prophets influenced King Ahab of Israel and brought him to disgrace:

"Three years passed without war between Syria and Israel. In the third year Jehoshaphat king of Judah went down to the king of Israel. The king of Israel said to his officers, Do you not know that Ramoth-gilead is ours, and we care not for her to take her out of the hand of the king of Syria? Then he said to Jehoshaphat, Will you go with me to Ramoth-gilead? He is like your people, my horses are like your horses." And Jehoshaphat said to the king of Israel, "Consult the word of the LORD, I pray you today." Then the king of Israel gathered together the prophets, about four hundred men, and said to them, "Shall I go to battle against Ramoth-gilead, or shall I desist?" from Israel to Jehoshaphat: There is yet one man by whom we may inquire of the LORD: but I hate him, because he never prophesies good concerning me, but always evil; is Micaiah the son of Imlah. Jehoshaphat said, Let not the king speak thus. Then the king of Israel called an officer and said to him, Quickly bring Micaiah the son of Imlah. Now the king of Israel and Jehoshaphat the king of Judah were sitting, each on his throne, dressed in royal attire, in a field at the entrance to the gate of Samaria; and all the prophets prophesied before them. Zedekiah the son of Chenaanah had made horns of iron, and said, Thus saith the LORD, With these thou shalt smite the Syrians until thou hast consumed them. And all the prophets prophesied the same thing, saying, Go up to Ramoth-gilead, and you will succeed, for the Lord will deliver it into the king's hand. The messenger that went to call Micaiah said to him: Behold, with one voice the prophets have foretold success to the king; Let your word be like one of theirs, and speak what is good. Micaiah said, "As the Lord lives, whatever the Lord says to me, that will I speak."(1 Kings 22:1-14)

In this passage, the king of Israel, Ahab, approached the king of Judah, Jehoshaphat, to participate in a battle at Ramoth-gilead. Before making any decision, Jehoshaphat asked to consult the word of the Lord through the prophets.

Ahab gathered about four hundred prophets, who prophesied that the battle would be successful and that the Lord would deliver Ramoth-gilead into the king's hands. However, Jehoshaphat felt that something was wrong and asked if there were any prophets of the Lord who had not yet been consulted.

119

Ahab mentioned Micaiah, son of Imlah, but warned that he never prophesied good for him. Jehoshaphat insisted that the prophet be called, and the messenger who brought him encouraged Micaiah to speak what was pleasing to kings, just as the other prophets had done.

However, Micaiah replied that he would only speak what the Lord told him. When he arrived before the kings, he sarcastically prophesied that the battle would be a success and the kings would triumph. But when urged to speak the truth, Micaiah revealed the vision he saw in heaven: he saw the Lord asking who could deceive Ahab so that he would go up to Ramoth-gilead and fall in battle. A lying spirit volunteered to be that deceiver, and the Lord allowed him to seduce Ahab's prophets into prophesying victory, drawing him to his destruction.

This story highlights the dangerous influence of false prophets who band together to seduce leaders and people with pleasant words and messages that align with their desires. The crowd was led to believe the false prophecies that promised victory, while Micaiah remained faithful to divine truth, even if it resulted in disfavor for himself.

2 Peter 2:1-3 - False Prophets Among the People

The apostle Peter also warned of the presence of false prophets among the people, who propagate harmful teachings to gain followers and cause divisions:

"And there were also false prophets among the people, as there will also be false teachers among you, who will secretly bring in destructive heresies and deny the Lord who bought them, bringing sudden destruction upon themselves. And many will follow their dissipations, by whom the way of truth will be blasphemed;(2 Pedro 2:1-3)

In that passage, Peter warned of the presence of false prophets among the people, who would introduce destructive heresies, deny the Lord, and promote a dissolute lifestyle. These false prophets do not seek truth and holiness, but their own satisfaction and profit.

This warning is timeless and remains relevant today. Sadly, there are still people who present themselves as religious or spiritual leaders, but whose motives are questionable and whose doctrines are distorted. It is our duty as believers to discern these misleading teachings and hold fast to the truth of Scripture.

121

Matthew 7:15-20 - Recognizing False Prophets by Their Fruits

Jesus also gave us clear teaching on how to recognize false prophets:

"Beware of false prophets, which come to you in sheep's clothing, but inwardly they are ravening wolves. By their fruit you will know them. Do they gather grapes from thornbushes or figs from thistles? So every good tree bears good fruit, but a bad tree bears bad fruit. A good tree cannot bear bad fruit, nor can a bad tree bear good fruit. Every tree that does not bear good fruit is cut down and thrown into the fire. Therefore by their fruits you will know them."(Matthew 7:15-20)

Jesus warns us to be on the lookout for false prophets who masquerade as good people but whose intentions are evil. They may appear harmless and friendly on the outside, but their true character is revealed through their actions and teachings.

Just as a tree is recognized by the fruit it produces, false prophets are identified by the consequences of their words and actions. If their doctrines lead people into sin, division, and estrangement from God, we can be sure they are false prophets.

On the other hand, true prophets and spiritual leaders produce fruits of love, peace, justice and holiness. They promote unity and encourage people to follow the truth and draw closer to God.

THE JOURNEY OF RECONSTRUCTION

After the fall, some of these preachers will have the opportunity to rebuild their lives and their beliefs. Through learning from adversity, they will understand the importance of cultivating an intimate connection with God, strengthening themselves to resist the wiles of false gods.

Repentance and the Search for God

When a preacher falls prey to false gods and prophets, the first step on the journey of rebuilding is repentance. Recognizing the mistakes made and turning to God in humility is essential to start rebuilding faith and relationship with the Lord.

The Bible offers us countless stories of characters who faced falls and sincerely repented. A striking example is King David, a man after God's own heart, but who fell into adultery with Bathsheba and plotted the death of Uriah, her husband. David, when confronted by the prophet Nathan, acknowledged his sins and sought God's forgiveness with a repentant heart. Psalm 51, written by David after this episode, is a powerful prayer of repentance and seeking restoration:

"Have mercy on me, O God, according to Your lovingkindness; blot out my transgressions, according to the multitude of Your mercies. Wash me thoroughly from my iniquity, and cleanse me from my sin. For I know my transgressions, and my sin is always before me. My mother conceived. Behold, You love truth in the inmost parts, and in the secret place You make me to know wisdom. Purify me with hyssop, and I will be clean; wash me, and I will be whiter than snow. Make me hear joy and gladness, that the bones you have crushed may rejoice. Hide the face of my sins, and blot out all my iniquities. Create in me a pure heart, O God, and renew a steadfast spirit within me. Cast me not out of your presence and do not take your Holy Spirit from me, restore to me the joy of your salvation and sustain me with a willing spirit. Then I will teach transgressors your ways, and sinners will return to you. Deliver me from bloodshed, O God, the God of my salvation, and my tongue will praise your righteousness highly. Open my lips, Lord, and my mouth will proclaim your praise. For you do not desire sacrifices; otherwise I would give them away; you do not delight in burnt offerings. The sacrifices of God are a broken spirit; a broken and contrite heart, O God, you will not despise. Do good to Zion, according to your good pleasure; builds the walls of Jerusalem. Then shalt thou be pleased with the sacrifices of righteousness, with burnt offerings and burnt offerings; Then bulls will be offered on your altar." (Salmo 51:1-19)

This Psalm expresses David's deep sorrow for his sins and his plea for forgiveness and restoration. The rebuilding journey begins with sincerely acknowledging mistakes and reaching out to God for mercy and restoration.

Refuge in the Word of God

After repentance, the next step on the rebuilding journey is to find refuge in God's word. The Bible is an inexhaustible source of wisdom, guidance, and comfort for those seeking spiritual strength.

Psalm 119 is the longest chapter in the Bible and is dedicated to the beauty and power of God's word. In his verses, the psalmist expresses his love for the law of the Lord and its importance in his life:

"How would I love your law! It is my meditation all day long. You have made me wiser than my enemies through your commandments; for I have them always with me. I have more understanding than all my teachers, because I meditate on your testimonies. I am more prudent than the aged, because I keep your precepts. I have turned my feet away from every evil way to observe your word. I have not departed from your judgments, because you have taught me. your words! Sweeter than honey to my mouth. By your commandments I have gained understanding; therefore I hate every false way. Your word is a lamp to my feet, and a light to my path. (Salmo 119:97-106)

This Psalm shows how the word of God is valued by the psalmist and how it has been a constant source of wisdom and guidance in his life. Likewise, those seeking to rebuild their faith and beliefs must immerse themselves in the Scriptures, meditate on its teachings and apply them in their rebuilding journey.

Through reading the Bible, preachers can understand God's true will, learn from the experiences of biblical characters and find encouragement in divine promises. The word of God is like a light that illuminates the path of those who seek to strengthen their faith and discernment.

Deepening Prayer and Communion with God

Prayer and communion with God are fundamental pillars in the journey of spiritual reconstruction. Through prayer, preachers can communicate directly with the Lord, voice their concerns, seek guidance, and find solace in times of trouble.

The Bible encourages us to pray without ceasing and to bring all our worries and anxieties before God:

"Do not be anxious about anything, but in everything, by prayer and petition, with thanksgiving, make your requests known to God." (Philippians 4:6)

Jesus also taught us to pray sincerely and intimately, with a heart turned to God:

"This is how you therefore pray: Our Father who art in heaven, hallowed be your name; your kingdom come, your will be done, on earth as it is in heaven; give us this day our daily bread; and forgive us our debts, as we forgive our debtors; and lead us not into temptation; but deliver us from evil, for yours is the kingdom, and the power, and the glory forever. Amen."(Matthew 6:9-13)

Prayer connects us directly with God and strengthens our faith and trust in Him. Through fellowship with the Lord, preachers can find solace in their struggles and be empowered by the Holy Spirit to discern truth from the lies of false prophets.

Learning from the Lessons of the Past

A crucial part of the rebuilding journey is learning from the lessons of the past, both from biblical characters and historical events that teach us about the consequences of following false gods and prophets.

A significant example is the history of Israel in the Old Testament. The people of Israel experienced cycles of obeying and disobeying God, being seduced by pagan gods and false prophets. On many occasions, God sent true prophets to warn them and call them to repentance, but the nation often rejected their messages.

A notable example is the story of the prophet Elijah and the challenge on Mount Carmel. Elijah confronted the prophets of Baal and challenged them to prove that their god was real. They prayed in vain, but the God of Israel answered Elijah's request by consuming the sacrifice with fire from heaven. The episode highlights the superiority of the true God over false gods and shows the consequences of following the paths of falsehood.

Another example is the story of the prophet Jeremiah, who faced opposition from false prophets who prophesied peace and prosperity for Jerusalem, while God was warning of impending destruction due to the people's disobedience and idolatry. Jeremiah was persecuted and rejected for his messages, but he remained faithful to God's word, even in the face of suffering and challenges.

Through these stories, preachers on the journey of rebuilding can learn the devastating consequences of falsehood and the blessings of obedience and the pursuit of divine truth. These lessons from the past serve as a guide for the present, enabling you to discern the wiles of false gods and choose to follow God's truth.

Strengthening Spiritual Discernment

The rebuilding journey also requires strengthening spiritual discernment. Discernment is the ability to distinguish between truth and error, good and evil, and is critical to avoiding the pitfalls of false prophets.

The Bible encourages us to seek God's discernment and wisdom in our lives:

"If your heart is wise, then my heart will rejoice, and so will I. My kidneys will rejoice when your lips speak what is right." (Proverbs 23:15-16)

"If anyone lacks wisdom, let him ask God, who gives liberally and does not reproach, and it will be given him." (James 1:5)

Through prayer, study of God's word, and constant search for divine wisdom, preachers can strengthen their spiritual discernment and be aware of the lies of false prophets. The Holy Ghost is our guide and comforter, enabling us to discern truth and follow God's way.

The importance of monitoring and community support

In the journey of reconstruction, it is crucial to have the support and accompaniment of a faith community. Having brothers and sisters who share the same faith and are concerned about each other's spiritual well-being can be a source of encouragement, comfort, and responsibility.

The Bible encourages us to help each other and strengthen each other in the faith:

"Therefore exhort one another, and build one another up, even as ye also do."(1 Thessalonians 5:11)

"Brothers, if a man is overtaken in any trespass, you who are spiritual restore such a one in a spirit of gentleness; taking heed to yourself, lest you also be tempted."(Galatians 6:1)

Community support and monitoring can be a determining factor in the journey of reconstruction. Having people who pray with us, study the word of God with us, share experiences and offer emotional support can make all the difference in our journey of spiritual growth.

THE SEARCH FOR DISCERNMENT

The search for discernment becomes essential in this journey. In this chapter, we will learn about the teachings of wise counselors and spiritual guides who help the faithful to deepen their understanding of the scriptures and discern between the voices that echo in their hearts.

The Importance of Spiritual Discernment

Spiritual discernment is a valuable skill for believers, especially when faced with the presence of false prophets and misleading teachings. The apostle Paul exhorts us to seek this discernment in his letters:

"Examine everything. Hold fast to the good." (1 Thessalonians 5:21)

"Now, discernment is not simply knowing the difference between right and wrong, but it is the ability to understand spiritual matters in depth, judge wisely, and live in accordance with God's truth.

The Wisdom of Counselors

In seeking discernment, it is valuable to seek guidance from wise and experienced counselors in the faith. In the Bible, we find countless examples of men and women who acted as spiritual guides and counselors for the faithful.

A notable example is King Solomon, known for his God-given wisdom. In 1 Kings 3:9-12, Solomon asks God for wisdom to govern the people of Israel, and the Lord grants him incomparable wisdom:

"Give therefore thy servant an understanding heart to judge thy people, that he may discern between good and evil; for who is able to judge this thy great people? And it pleased the Lord that Solomon asked this thing. Behold, I give you a wise and understanding heart, so that before you there was none like you, nor after you shall there be another like you."

Solomon's wisdom made him a valuable advisor to the people of Israel. His wise teachings and decisions reflected God's presence in his life, and his example teaches us to seek divine wisdom in our choices and discernments.

Paul's Example as a Spiritual Counselor

Another striking example in the Bible is the apostle Paul, who acted as a spiritual advisor to various Christian communities. Paul was a man of great knowledge of the Scriptures and the gospel of Jesus Christ. His wisdom and authority as an apostle made him a reference for the first Christians.

In his letters, Paul offers valuable teaching and advice for the communities he served. In Ephesians 1:17-18, Paul shares a prayer he prays for the Ephesians, asking God to grant them a spirit of wisdom and revelation in the full knowledge of God:

"That the God of our Lord Jesus Christ, the Father of glory, may give you the spirit of wisdom and revelation in the knowledge of him, to enlighten the eyes of your heart, that you may know what is the hope of his calling, what are the riches of the glory of his inheritance in the saints."

Paul not only shared teachings, but also sought to have the faithful grow in their spiritual discernment and knowledge of God. His example as a spiritual counselor shows us the importance of seeking guidance from experienced spiritual leaders in the journey of faith.

The Prayer for Discernment

Prayer plays a key role in the quest for discernment. As we seek God in prayer, we can ask for wisdom, discernment and clarity to understand divine truths and recognize the lies of false prophets.

In Proverbs 2:3-6, we find a call to seek discernment through prayer and the study of the word of God:

"Yes, if you cry out for understanding, and lift up your voice for understanding, if you seek wisdom like silver and seek her as for hid treasures, then you will understand the fear of the Lord and find the knowledge of God. For the Lord gives wisdom; from his mouth come knowledge and understanding."

Prayer is a powerful practice that connects us directly with God. When we seek discernment through prayer, we are acknowledging our dependence on God to understand the truth and protect us from the snares of falsehood.

The Role of the Holy Spirit in Discernment

The Holy Spirit plays a crucial role in the quest for spiritual discernment. He is our guide and comforter, enabling us to discern the truth and resist the temptations of the evil one.

In John 16:13, Jesus promises to send the Holy Spirit as our guide:

"When he, the Spirit of truth, comes, he will guide you into all the truth; for he will not speak on his own, but whatever he hears he will speak, and he will declare to you the things that are to come."

The Holy Ghost enables us to understand spiritual truths and discern between truth and error. He teaches, consoles, exhorts, and guides us on our journey of faith.

The Quest for Knowledge of the Scriptures

A fundamental way to seek discernment is through a knowledge of the Scriptures. The Bible is the word of God and contains all the wisdom and truth necessary for our spiritual life.

In 2 Timothy 3:16-17, Paul teaches the importance of the Scriptures:

"All Scripture is inspired by God and profitable for teaching, for reproof, for correction, for training in righteousness, that the man of God may be complete, equipped for every good work."

Studying the Scriptures helps us discern God's will, understand His teachings, and identify false teachings that can lead us astray. When we delve into the word of God, we are strengthened in our faith and able to discern between the voices that echo in our hearts.

The Danger of Self-Reliance

In our quest for discernment, it is important that we recognize our own limitations and dependence on God. Self-sufficiency and overconfidence in our own wisdom can make us vulnerable to the deceptions of false prophets.

The book of Proverbs warns us of man's wisdom that seems right but is actually based on his own understanding:

"There is a way that seems right to a man, but the end of it is the way of death." (Proverbs 14:12)

Pride and self-sufficiency can distance us from dependence on God and lead us to follow our own convictions, even when they

138

are at odds with the divine will. Therefore, it is important to recognize our need to seek God's wisdom and discernment in all areas of our lives.

The Example of the Bereans

In the search for discernment, the example of the Bereans in Acts 17:11 it's inspiring:

"And immediately the brethren sent Paul and Silas away by night to Berea; and when they arrived there, they went into the synagogue of the Jews. Now these from Berea were more noble than those from Thessalonica; for they received the word with all eagerness, examining the Scriptures daily to see whether these things were so."

The Bereans did not blindly accept the apostles' teaching, but sought to check the Scriptures daily to discern the truthfulness of the teachings presented to them. This example teaches us not to take any teaching lightly and to carefully examine God's word to discern the truth.

Communion with the Church

Another important aspect in the search for discernment is communion with the church. The church is a body of believers who seek to follow Christ and live according to his teachings.

Fellowship with other Christians can enrich us with different perspectives and faith experiences.

In Hebrews 10:25, we are encouraged not to forsake the fellowship of the church:

"Let us not give up meeting together, as some are in the habit of doing, but encourage one another, and all the more as you see the Day approaching."

Through fellowship with other Christians, we can share our spiritual doubts, struggles, and quests, empowering each other on the journey of discernment and spiritual growth.

The Search for Truth

Finally, the pursuit of discernment requires a commitment to the truth. We must be diligent in our pursuit of God's truth, willing to abandon any teaching that is not in line with God's word.

In 2 Timothy 2:15, Paul exhorts to seek God's approval, being "a workman who does not need to be ashamed, rightly handling the word of truth."

In seeking discernment, it is critical to be open to correction and constant learning. We must be willing to change our understanding and convictions as we are enlightened by the word of God and the Holy Spirit.

THE TRAPS OF THE EGO

Ego can be a treacherous enemy, leading preachers to seek personal glory at the expense of true worship. In this chapter, we'll explore the challenges of keeping the ego in check and the importance of humility in hearing God's genuine voice.

The Ego and Its Influence on the Spiritual Journey

Ego, broadly speaking, refers to the sense of self-importance, the individual "I" that seeks recognition, success, and validation. On the spiritual journey, the ego can be a powerful force, capable of diverting us from our true purpose of worshiping God and serving others. When not controlled, the ego can corrupt the heart and lead the preacher to fall into the traps of vanity and the pursuit of personal glory.

In Proverbs 16:18, we find a warning about pride, which is closely linked to the ego:

"Pride goes before ruin, and a haughty spirit before a fall."

Seeking recognition and ego satisfaction can lead us away from true worship of God, diverting our attention from God's will to our own selfish ambitions and desires. It is important, therefore, to recognize the ego's negative influence on our spiritual journey and to seek humility as an antidote to these pitfalls.

The Example of John the Baptist

In the New Testament, we find a remarkable example of humility and submission to God's will in John the Baptist. He was called to be the forerunner of Jesus Christ, preparing the way for the Messiah. Despite having a high position in his mission, John the Baptist demonstrated a deep humility and a clear understanding of his role as a servant of God.

In John 3:30, John the Baptist humbly declares:

"He needs to increase and I need to decrease."

This simple sentence reflects the attitude of a humble heart, willing to give up protagonism so that the glory of God prevails. John the Baptist understood that his mission was to point to Christ and not to himself. He did not seek fame or personal recognition, but only to serve God and fulfill the purpose entrusted to him.

Jesus' Warning about the Self

Jesus also taught about the importance of humility and service to others. In Matthew 20:25-28, He confronts the selfishness of the disciples who sought prominent positions in the kingdom of heaven:

"You know that the rulers of the peoples rule over them, and their great ones exercise authority over them. It will not be so among you; rather, whoever wishes to be great among you shall be your servant; and whoever wishes to be first among you shall be your servant; just as the Son of Man did not come to be served, but to serve, and to give his life as a ransom for many."

Jesus teaches us that greatness in the kingdom of God is not related to power, position or seeking personal recognition, but to service and humility. The true spiritual leader is the one who puts himself at the service of others, following the example of Christ, who came into the world to serve and give his life as a ransom for humanity.

The Quest for Human Approval

The quest for approval and recognition from others is one of the most common pitfalls of the ego. The desire to be praised and admired can lead preachers to compromise the true worship of God, seeking to please men instead of obeying divine commands.

In Galatians 1:10, Paulo reflects on the search for human approval:

"Why do I now persuade men or God? Or do I try to please men? If I were still pleasing men, I would not be a servant of Christ."

Paul reminds us that our allegiance must be in God and His teachings, not diverted by human praise or criticism. Pleasing God must be our main objective, even if it means displeasing men.

The Temptation of Spiritual Pride

Spiritual pride is another dangerous trap of the ego. When a preacher falls into this trap, he begins to believe that he is superior to others in terms of spirituality, knowledge, or divine revelation. This feeling of superiority can lead to arrogance and judgment of others, alienating the preacher from the true spirit of love and humility that should permeate the Christian life.

In Romans 12:3, Paul warns us about the danger of spiritual pride:

"For by the grace given to me I say to each one of you not to think more highly of yourself than is convenient, but to think soberly of yourself, in accordance with the measure of faith which God has apportioned to each one."

Paul reminds us that the grace and spiritual gifts we receive are not reasons to be puffed up, but to serve others with humility and love.

Humility as an Antidote to the Ego

Humility is the essential antidote to combating the pitfalls of the ego on the spiritual journey. Humility helps us recognize our dependence on God, our imperfection, and our constant need for growth and transformation.

In James 4:6, we find an important truth about humility:

"Rather, he gives greater grace. Therefore he says, God resists the proud, but gives grace to the humble."

When we humble ourselves before God, He gives us grace and wisdom to discern His will and resist the temptations of self. Humility allows us to recognize our weaknesses and seek the strength and divine direction to overcome them.

The Importance of Self-Assessment

Self-assessment is a valuable practice for combating ego traps. When we honestly assess ourselves, we can identify possible traces of vanity, pride or the search for personal recognition in our actions and motivations.

In 1 Corinthians 11:28, Paul encourages us to self-assess in relation to participation in the Lord's Supper:

"Let a man examine himself, and so eat of this bread and drink of this cup."

This self-assessment is a reminder that our spiritual journey requires honesty and humility to recognize our weaknesses and seek God's grace to overcome them.

The Power of Transforming Grace

The power of God's transforming grace is essential in the pursuit of humility. When we recognize our weaknesses and seek His grace, we are enabled to overcome the pitfalls of the ego and grow in our faith.

In 2 Corinthians 12:9-10, Paul relates an experience in which God gave him His grace to deal with his weaknesses:

"(...) my grace is sufficient for you, because power is perfected in weakness. Therefore, I will gladly rather boast about my weaknesses, so that the power of Christ may rest upon me.

Paul recognized his weakness and sought God's grace to overcome it. This experience teaches us that humility is not a sign of weakness, but a recognition of our constant need for God's grace.

Learning from Weaknesses

Weaknesses can be valuable opportunities to learn important lessons and develop humility in our lives. When we sincerely face our weaknesses and seek God's guidance, we are perfected in our faith and empowered to serve with greater love and compassion.

In 2 Corinthians 12:9, Paul learns from his weaknesses:

"Wherefore I take pleasure in infirmities, in injuries, in necessities, in persecutions, in distresses, for Christ's sake. For when I am weak, then am I strong."

Paul understood that his weaknesses brought him closer to God and made him stronger in His grace. Thus, learning from our weaknesses helps us grow in humility and dependence on God.

The Continuing Journey of Humility

The journey of humility is continuous and requires a constant search for God's presence in our lives. Through prayer, meditation on the Scriptures, and sincere self-examination, we can cultivate humility in our hearts and combat the pitfalls of the ego.

In 1 Pedro 5:5-6, Peter exhorts us to seek humility:

"Likewise, you younger ones, be subject to your elders.

May every preacher and believer strive to cultivate humility in their spiritual journey, recognizing the need to depend on God and seek His will above their own ambitions. Humility draws us closer to God and makes us more sensitive to His voice, allowing us to hear and obey His leading in our lives and ministries.

THE REDISCOVERY OF TRUE FAITH

Through experiences of overcoming and self-knowledge, preachers who deviated from the true faith will be able to rediscover the true purpose of their vocation. The scars of the past will become powerful testimonies of the importance of standing firm in the faith.

149

The Journey of Overcoming

Those who have fallen into the traps of the ego and strayed from true faith may face a journey of overcoming to rediscover their true purpose and reconnect with God. Overcoming involves acknowledging past mistakes, sincerely repenting, and seeking reconciliation with God and others.

In Romans 3:23, Paul reminds us that all have sinned and fall short of the glory of God:

"For all have sinned and fall short of the glory of God;"

This humble understanding of our sinful nature is essential for us to recognize the need for redemption and overcoming in our lives.

The Power of Regret

Genuine repentance is an important step in the journey of rediscovering true faith. Repentance means changing direction, turning from sin and turning to God for forgiveness and restoration.

In Acts 3:19, Peter exhorts the people to repentance:

"Repent ye therefore, and be converted, that your sins may be blotted out."

The power of repentance lies in the possibility of a new life, a life reconciled with God and His will. For preachers who have fallen into the traps of self, repentance will lead to a rediscovery of true faith and a reaffirmation of their call to serve God.

The Quest for Divine Forgiveness

The quest for divine forgiveness is a fundamental part of the process of rediscovering true faith. Recognizing our weaknesses and shortcomings, we approach God with contrite hearts, seeking His grace and mercy.

In 1 John 1:9, we find a promise of pardon:

"If we confess our sins, He is faithful and just to forgive us our sins and to cleanse us from all unrighteousness."

Sincere confession of our sins and seeking God's forgiveness are essential to restoring our faith and relationship with Him. By experiencing divine forgiveness, preachers who have strayed from the faith can find hope and renewal for their journey of rediscovery.

The Role of the Christian Community

The Christian community plays an important role in rediscovering true faith for preachers facing this journey. The support, prayer, and guidance of brothers and sisters in Christ can be instrumental in helping preachers get back on their feet and continue in their calling.

In Galatians 6:1-2, Paul exhorts us to fellowship and mutual support:

"Brothers, if a man is overtaken in any trespass, you who are spiritual restore such a one in a spirit of meekness, taking heed to yourself, lest you also be tempted. Bear one another's burdens, and so fulfill the law of Christ."

The Christian community can be a place of healing, encouragement, and spiritual growth for those who are looking to rediscover their true faith. It is an environment where God's love can be experienced through mutual care and compassion.

The Importance of Self-Acceptance

Self-acceptance is a crucial aspect of the journey of rediscovering true faith. As preachers face their weaknesses and failures, it is important that they also allow themselves to accept their imperfections and learn from them.

In 2 Corinthians 12:9, Paul shares God's response to his weaknesses:

"(...) My grace is sufficient for you, because power is perfected in weakness. Therefore, I will gladly rather boast about my weaknesses, so that the power of Christ may rest upon me."

Accepting our weaknesses with humility does not mean conforming to them, but recognizing that God's grace is sufficient to strengthen us and enable us to continue in His will. By accepting themselves and trusting in the grace of God, preachers can rediscover their true identity in Christ and their calling to serve Him.

The Wisdom of Learning

Experiences of deviation from the true faith can be valuable learning opportunities. By reflecting on past mistakes, preachers can gain wisdom and insight to avoid the same pitfalls in the future.

In Proverbs 9:9, we find an incentive to seek knowledge and wisdom:

"Give instruction to the wise, and he will become wiser; teach the righteous, and he will grow in understanding."

Through learning from their own experiences and teaching the word of God, preachers can mature in their faith and discernment, rediscovering their vocation with greater wisdom and dedication.

The Valuation of Scars

The scars of the past can be powerful testimonies of God's grace and power in our lives. Instead of being ashamed of their failures, preachers can treasure their scars as evidence of their journey of rediscovery and transformation.

In 2 Corinthians 1:3-4, Paul shares how God comforts us in our afflictions, so that we can comfort those who are going through similar situations:

"Blessed be the God and Father of our Lord Jesus Christ, the Father of mercies and the God of all comfort, who comforts us in all our tribulation, that we may be able to comfort those who are in any trouble, with the comfort with which we ourselves are comforted by God."

Scars can be a source of comfort and inspiration to others, showing that even in the face of mistakes and failures, God's grace is sufficient to restore us and equip us for His work.

The Purpose of the Trial

Experiences of deviation from the true faith can be seen as trials designed to strengthen and refine the preachers' faith. By facing the consequences of their choices and seeking restoration in God, preachers can emerge stronger and more dedicated in their spiritual journey.

In James 1:2-4, we are encouraged to view trials as opportunities for growth:

"Consider it all joy, my brothers, when you fall into various temptations, knowing that the testing of your faith works patience. But let patience have its perfect work, that you may be perfect and complete, lacking nothing."

This perspective teaches us to value trials as part of the process of growth and spiritual maturity, allowing us to rediscover true faith even in adversity.

The Quest for Intimacy with God

Intimacy with God is a fundamental aspect in rediscovering true faith. As they draw closer to God for restoration and direction, preachers will find a deeper connection with the Creator that will guide them on their spiritual journey.

In Jeremiah 29:13, God encourages us to seek Him with all our hearts:

"And ye shall seek me, and find me, when ye seek me with all your heart."

By dedicating themselves to seeking God with all their hearts, preachers will find the strength and direction needed to rediscover their true faith and establish themselves in their calling as servants of God.

The Importance of Persistence

The journey of rediscovering true faith can be challenging and require persistence. However, as preachers persevere in their pursuit of God and dedication to the true faith, they will reap the fruits of spiritual growth and renewal.

In Galatians 6:9, we are encouraged not to be discouraged:

"And let us not be weary in doing good, for in due season we shall reap, if we do not faint."

Persistence in seeking God and holding fast to the true faith will bring rewards in His time. Preachers who faced overcoming and self-knowledge in their journey of rediscovery can testify how God transformed and restored them, making their lives and ministries even more impactful for the Kingdom of God.

THE ILLUMINATED PATH

On the last leg of this journey, we will accompany preachers who, renewed in their faith and discernment, will become enlightened guides for their communities. United by humility and acquired wisdom, they will share the true divine message, warning about the dangers of false gods and leading hearts to authentic and pure worship.

157

The Renewal of Faith

The rediscovery of true faith brought a profound spiritual renewal to preachers who faced the journey of overcoming and self-knowledge. This renewal is an ongoing process as preachers surrender more and more to God's will and seek His presence in their lives and ministries.

In Romans 12:2, Paul exhorts us to be transformed by the renewing of our minds:

"And do not be conformed to this world, but be transformed by the renewing of your mind, that you may prove what God's will is, that which is good and acceptable and perfect."

Renewing the mind is essential for preachers to discern God's will and become enlightened guides in their communities.

The Discernment of Truth

Preachers renewed in their faith acquire a keen insight into divine truth. By immersing themselves in the Scriptures and cultivating a deeper intimacy with God, they are able to clearly identify false doctrines and the wiles of false gods.

In 1 John 4:1, John admonishes us to test the spirits to discern the truth:

158

"Beloved, believe not every spirit, but try the spirits whether they are of God, because many false prophets are gone out into the world."

This discernment is crucial for them to lead their communities safely and firmly on the path of truth.

The Testimony of Forgiveness

Preachers who have experienced the journey of rediscovering true faith also have powerful testimonies of God's forgiveness and grace. Their stories of overcoming and restoration are living examples of God's unconditional love and His ability to transform lives.

In Ephesians 1:7, Paul celebrates forgiveness and redemption in Christ:

"In whom we have redemption through his blood, the forgiveness of sins, according to the riches of his grace."

This witness of forgiveness inspires and encourages their communities to seek reconciliation with God and embrace the true faith with humility and gratitude.

Guidance in the Word

As enlightened guides, preachers now strive to guide their communities in the Word of God. Their preaching and teaching are grounded in Scripture, and they share divine truth with clarity and conviction.

In 2 Timothy 3:16-17, Paul emphasizes the importance of the Scriptures for teaching and guidance:

"All Scripture is given by inspiration of God, and is profitable for teaching, for reproof, for correction, for training in righteousness, that the man of God may be complete, equipped for every good work."

Enlightened preachers understand that the Word of God is an inexhaustible source of wisdom and guidance for their lives and ministries.

The Warning Against False Gods

With their renewed wisdom and discernment, preachers are now on the alert to warn their communities of the dangers of false gods and false doctrines. They identify the signs of false prophets and instruct their faithful to guard against the seductions of the world.

160

In 2 Pedro 2:1, Peter warns about false teachers who introduce destructive heresies:

"As among the people there will also be false teachers, who will secretly introduce destructive heresies, and will deny the Lord who bought them, bringing sudden destruction upon themselves."

Enlightened preachers are vigilant in defending the truth and protecting their communities from the influence of false gods.

Authentic and Pure Worship

With their hearts renewed and their eyes fixed on God's truth, enlightened preachers lead their communities in authentic and pure worship. They encourage their faithful to worship God in spirit and in truth, seeking an intimate connection with the Creator.

In John 4:23-24, Jesus talks about true worship:

"But the hour is coming, and now is, when the true worshipers will worship the Father in spirit and in truth; for the Father seeks such to worship him. God is Spirit, and those who worship him must worship in spirit and truth."

Enlightened preachers lead their communities into a deeper and more meaningful worship experience, where hearts are turned wholly to God.

The Unity in Truth

Enlightened preachers also seek to promote unity within their communities based on true faith and the principles of love and compassion. They know that unity among the faithful is fundamental to the effective witness of the gospel to the world.

In Ephesians 4:3, Paul emphasizes the importance of unity in the bond of peace:

"Seeking to keep the unity of the Spirit in the bond of peace."

Unity actually strengthens the Christian community and makes it more resistant to the onslaught of false gods and divisions.

Accompanying New Converts

Enlightened preachers take special care of new converts, accompanying them on their journey of faith and discipleship. They are caring guides, sharing their personal experiences and guiding you in spiritual growth.

In Matthew 28:19-20, Jesus commissions His disciples to make disciples of all nations:

"Therefore go, teach all nations, baptizing them in the name of the Father, and of the Son, and of the Holy Spirit; teaching them to observe all things that I have commanded you; and, lo, I am with you always, even to the end of the age. Amen."

Enlightened preachers fulfill this great commission by investing in the spiritual lives of new converts and helping them grow in Christ.

The Example of Humility

Humility is a hallmark of enlightened preachers. They recognize that they are God's servants and that their role is to be instruments in His hands. Your trust is in God's power and not your human abilities.

In Philippians 2:3-4, Paul exhorts us to practice humility:

"Do nothing through strife or vainglory, but in humility each esteem others better than themselves. Do not look each to his own, but each also to the things of others."

Enlightened preachers are models of humility for their communities, inspiring them to follow Christ's example.

Service with Love

Finally, enlightened preachers dedicate themselves to service with love and compassion. They have in their hearts a genuine desire to lead their communities to an encounter with God and to be instruments of His grace and mercy.

In 1 Pedro 4:10-11, Peter encourages us to serve one another with the gifts we have received from God:

"Each one administer to others the gift as he has received it, as good stewards of the manifold grace of God. If anyone speaks, speak in the words of God; if anyone administers, administer according to the power that God gives; so that in everything God may be glorified through Jesus Christ, to whom belong glory and power forever and ever. Amen."

Enlightened preachers serve with love and dedication, always seeking to glorify God in everything they do.

THE SIGNS OF TRUTH

Just as the seasons of the year bring with them unmistakable signs, the words of the Lord also carry unique characteristics. Through inspiring examples, we will learn to recognize the signs of true prophecy, enabling us to reject the false promises of presumptuous prophets.

Prophecy Fulfilled: Sign of Authenticity

One of the distinguishing features of the Lord's words is their fulfillment. When God speaks, His Word is true and infallible, and His promises are fulfilled at the right time and beyond dispute.

In Isaiah 55:11, God declares, "So shall my word be that goes forth from my mouth; it shall not return to me empty, but shall accomplish what I please, and shall prosper in the thing for which I sent it."

In Isaiah 7:14, the prophet Isaiah predicted the coming of the Messiah, who would be conceived by a virgin: "Therefore the Lord himself will give you a sign: behold, the virgin will conceive, and give birth to a son, and will call his name Immanuel."

This prophecy was fulfilled in an extraordinary way when Jesus was born of Mary, the virgin, as recorded in Matthew 1:22-23: "All this took place to fulfill what the Lord had spoken through the prophet: 'The virgin will conceive and give birth to a son, and they will call his name Immanuel' which means 'God with us'."

The exact fulfillment of prophecies is a clear sign of their authenticity and divine origin.

166

Consistency with Scripture: Harmony in Revelation

God's true words do not contradict His previous revelation. The biblical canon is a coherent and harmonious set of teachings, and any subsequent revelation must conform to what has already been revealed.

In 2 Timothy 3:16-17, Paul writes about the importance of the Scriptures as a rule of faith:

"All Scripture is given by inspiration of God, and is profitable for teaching, for reproof, for correction, for training in righteousness, that the man of God may be complete, equipped for every good work."

True prophets do not deviate from the central message of the Bible, but faithfully reinforce and clarify its teachings.

The Glory of God: Focus of Prophecy

True prophecies are primarily intended to glorify God and not to exalt the prophet or satisfy your selfish desires. The glory of God must be at the heart of divine revelations, directing the hearts of the faithful to worship and obedience.

In Revelation 19:10, John emphasizes the purpose of the prophecies: "Then I fell at his feet to worship him, but he said to me, See, do not do that; I am your fellow servant, and of your

167

brothers, who have the testimony of Jesus. Worship God; for the testimony of Jesus is the spirit of prophecy."

True prophecy points to and testifies to Jesus Christ as the Son of God and Savior of mankind, leading people to turn to Him in worship and surrender.

The Lead to Repentance and Holiness

The Lord's words bring a message of repentance and holiness, inviting the faithful to turn away from sin and seek a life of righteousness before God.

In Acts 3:19-20, Peter calls people to repentance: "Repent therefore and be converted, that your sins may be blotted out, so that the times of refreshing may come from the presence of the Lord, and he may send Jesus Christ, who was preached to you before."

True prophecy confronts sin and invites hearts to be reconciled to God through sincere repentance and the pursuit of holiness.

The Fruit of the Spirit: Evidence of Authenticity

True prophecy produces the fruit of the Holy Spirit in the lives of those who receive it. In Galatians 5:22-23, Paul describes the fruits of the Spirit: "But the fruit of the Spirit is love, joy, peace, longsuffering, gentleness, goodness, faith, meekness, temperance."

When a prophecy is genuine, it brings with it the transforming power of the Holy Spirit, generating positive and lasting change in the lives of believers.

Confirmation by Extraordinary Means

On some occasions, God can confirm His words through extraordinary signs and wonders. These signs are further evidence that the revelation is genuine and comes from the Most High.

In Exodus 4:1-5, God confirmed Moses' call with miraculous signs:

"1 - Moses answered, They will not believe me, nor will they listen to my voice, because they will say, The Lord did not appear to you.

2 - The Lord asked him, What is that in your hand? He replied: A rod.

3 - Then he said to him, Throw it on the earth. He cast it to the earth, and it turned into a snake; and Moses fled from her.

4 - The Lord said to Moses, Reach out your hand and take hold of its tail - he reached out, took it by the tail, and it became a staff in his hand -

5 - that they may believe that the LORD, the God of their fathers, the God of Abraham, the God of Isaac, and the God of Jacob, has appeared to you."

However, it is important to note that not every sign or miracle is necessarily a confirmation of authenticity, as false prophets can also perform apparent miracles. Therefore, confirmation by extraordinary means must be considered in conjunction with the other signs of authenticity.

The Voice of the Good Shepherd: Knowing the Lord

In John 10:27, Jesus talks about the sheep's knowledge of his voice: "My sheep listen to my voice; I know them, and they follow me."

When we truly know the voice of the Good Shepherd, we are able to discern between truth and falsehood. Intimate knowledge of God and fellowship with Him through prayer and meditation on the Scriptures enable us to recognize His voice and protect us from the wiles of false prophets.

THE TEST OF TIME

The passage of time is one of the greatest tests of the authenticity of revelations. In this chapter, we will delve into stories of prophecies that have withstood the test of time and have undeniably been fulfilled, contrasting with the empty words that have faded over the years.

171

Isaiah's Prophecy of the Fall of Babylon

In Isaiah 13:17-19, the prophet Isaiah uttered a powerful prophecy about the fall of Babylon: "Behold, I will raise up against them the Medes, which will not care for silver, nor desire gold.

This prophecy has been amazingly fulfilled. In the year 539 B.C., Cyrus, the king of the Medes and Persians, conquered Babylon, as recorded in Daniel 5:30-31: "That same night Belshazzar the king of the Chaldeans was slain. Darius the Mede, about sixty-two years old, took the kingdom."

The fulfillment of this prophecy demonstrates the truth of Isaiah's words and God's sovereign action over the nations.

Ezekiel's Prophecy about Tire

The city of Tyre, famous for its wealth and maritime power, defied God in its arrogance. The prophet Ezekiel prophesied its destruction in Ezekiel 26:3-5:

"Therefore thus says the Lord GOD: Behold, I am against you, O Tyre, and will bring many nations against you, as the sea brings up its waves. And they shall break down the walls of Tire, and break down its towers; and I will scrape its dust, and make it a smooth rock; it shall be a stretch of nets to dry nets in

172

the midst of the sea, for I have spoken it, saith the Lord GOD; and it shall be spoil for the nations."

This prophecy was precisely fulfilled when Tire was besieged and destroyed by Alexander the Great in 332 BC. Afterwards, Tire was rebuilt on the mainland, as envisaged in Ezekiel 26:14.

The fulfillment of Ezekiel's prophecy about Tire is a stunning example of the accuracy of divine words and God's sovereign control about the destinies of nations.

The Prophecy of the Birth of Jesus in Bethlehem

One of the best-known Old Testament prophecies is about the birth of Jesus in Bethlehem, uttered by the prophet Micah. In Micah 5:2, it is written: "And you, Bethlehem-Ephrathah, too small to be numbered among the thousands of Judah, from you shall come forth to me the ruler of Israel, whose origin is from ancient times, from the days of eternity."

This prophecy was most notably fulfilled when Jesus was born in Bethlehem, as recorded in Matthew 2:1: "When Jesus was born in Bethlehem of Judah in the days of King Herod, behold, wise men from the East came to Jerusalem."

The fulfillment of this prophecy emphasizes God's faithfulness in fulfilling His promises and the centrality of Jesus in redemptive history.

Daniel's Prophecy of Successive World Powers

In Daniel 2:31-45, the prophet Daniel received a vision of a large statue representing four successive kingdoms that would rule the world:

"31 - You, O king, were looking, and behold, a great statue; this statue, which was immense, whose splendor was excellent, and it stood before you; and its appearance was terrible.

32 - The head of that statue was of fine gold; his breast and arms of silver; its belly and its thighs of bronze;

33 - the legs, of iron; his feet, part of iron and part of clay.

34 - You were watching this, when a stone was cut, without hands, which smote the statue in the feet of iron and clay and crushed them.

35 - Then the iron, the clay, the bronze, the silver, and the gold were broken to pieces together, and became like the chaff of the threshing floors in the summer, and the wind carried them away, and no trace of them was found. But the stone that struck the statue became a great mountain and filled the whole earth."

174

This prophecy was fulfilled with remarkable accuracy in the history of the world powers, represented by the different materials of the statue: the gold represented the Babylonian Empire, the silver the Medo-Persian Empire, the bronze the Greek Empire and the iron the Romans. The stone that destroys the statue represents the Kingdom of God, which is established through Jesus Christ.

The fulfillment of Daniel's prophecy about successive world powers is powerful evidence of God's sovereignty over human history and the accuracy of His prophetic words.

Jeremiah's Prophecy of Israel's Captivity and Return

In Jeremiah 25:11-12, the prophet Jeremiah uttered a prophecy about the captivity of Israel:

"All this land shall become a wilderness, an astonishment; and these nations shall serve the king of Babylon seventy years. And it shall come to pass, when the seventy years are accomplished, that I will punish the king of Babylon, and this nation, saith the Lord, by punishing their iniquity, and will punish the land of the Chaldeans, and will lay it in perpetual ruins."

This prophecy was exactly fulfilled when the people of Israel were taken into Babylonian captivity for seventy years.

In Daniel 9:2, Daniel, who was a contemporary of Jeremiah, recognized the fulfillment of this prophecy: "In the first year of his reign, I, Daniel, understood from the books that the number of years, which the Lord spoke to the prophet Jeremiah, in which the desolations of Jerusalem were to be accomplished, was seventy years."

In addition, in Jeremiah 29:10, the prophet also prophesied about the return of the people of Israel after the seventy years of captivity: "For thus says the Lord: When the seventy years are fulfilled in Babylon, I will visit you and fulfill my good word toward you, in bringing you back to this place."

This prophecy was also fulfilled when King Cyrus issued a decree allowing the people of Israel to return to their land and rebuild the temple, as recorded in Ezra 1:1-3.

The fulfillment of these prophecies by Jeremiah about Israel's captivity and return demonstrates the truthfulness of the prophetic words and God's faithfulness in fulfilling His promises.

Zechariah's Prophecy of Jesus' Triumphal Coming

In Zechariah 9:9, the prophet Zechariah uttered a prophecy about the triumphal coming of the Messiah: "Rejoice greatly, O daughter of Zion;

This prophecy was most notably fulfilled when Jesus rode into Jerusalem on a colt, as recorded in Matthew 21:4-5: "All this took place to fulfill what was spoken through the prophet: 'Say to the daughter of Zion, Behold, your King comes to you, lowly and riding on an ass, on a colt, the foal of a beast of burden.'"

The fulfillment of Zechariah's prophecy emphasizes the accuracy of divine words and the fulfillment of Messianic promises in Jesus Christ.

Jesus' Prophecy of the Destruction of the Temple

Jesus made a striking prophecy about the destruction of the temple in Jerusalem in Matthew 24:1-2: " And Jesus, leaving the temple, was withdrawing, when his disciples approached him to show him the buildings of the temple.

This prophecy was impressively fulfilled in A.D. 70, when the Roman army under Titus destroyed the Jerusalem temple, just as Jesus had predicted.

The fulfillment of Jesus' prophecy about the destruction of the temple is overwhelming proof of His deity and His knowledge of future events.

THE POWER OF PERSONAL EXPERIENCE

Personal experience is a reliable compass on the discernment journey. Through moving accounts, we will witness how the intimate encounter with the divine word molds the heart and strengthens the faith, enabling the faithful to distinguish between the Lord's genuine guidance and false speeches.

178

The Call of Samuel - 1 Samuel 3:1-10

The story of Samuel's call is a powerful example of the power of personal experience in discerning divine revelations. In 1 Samuel 3:1-10, we read:

"1 - The boy Samuel served the Lord before Eli; in those days the word of the Lord was very rare; visions were not frequent.

2 - But it happened one day, as Eli lay in his place and his eyes began to grow dim, so that he could no longer see,

3 - And Samuel was also lying in the temple of the Lord, where the ark of God was,

4 - Before the lamps of God went out, the Lord called Samuel, to which he replied: Here I am.

5 - So Eli ran and said to Samuel, Here I am, because you called me. But he said, I did not call you; go back to bed. And he went and lay down.

6 - The Lord called again: Samuel! And Samuel arose, and went to Eli, and said, Here I am, because you called me. Eli replied, I did not call you, my son; go back to bed.

7 - Now Samuel did not yet know the Lord, and the word of the Lord had not yet appeared to him.

8 - So the Lord called Samuel the third time, and he arose and went to Eli and said, Here I am, because you called me. So Eli understood that the Lord was calling the boy.

9 - Therefore Eli said to Samuel, Go, lie down; and if he calls you, you shall say, Speak, Lord, for your servant hears. So Samuel went and lay down in his place.

10 - The Lord came, stood there and called as at other times: Samuel, Samuel! He replied, Speak, Lord, for your servant hears."

In this narrative, we realize that Samuel did not initially recognize the voice of the Lord. Only after Eli's guidance did he learn to respond to the divine call. Samuel's personal experience of hearing and responding to the voice of God shaped his perception and enabled him to discern genuine revelations.

This story teaches us the importance of being sensitive to God's voice in our lives and how the personal experience of hearing and responding to Him can make us better able to distinguish between the Lord's true guidance and false speeches.

Saul's Encounter with Jesus - Acts 9:1-9

Another striking example of the power of personal experience in discernment is the story of Saul, who would later become the apostle Paul. In Acts 9:1-9, we find the account of Saul's encounter with Jesus on the way to Damascus:

"1 - Saul, still breathing threats and death against the disciples of the Lord, went to the high priest,

2 - And he asked him for letters to the synagogues in Damascus, so that if he found any on the Way, whether men or women, he might take them bound to Jerusalem.

3 - On his journey, as he approached Damascus, suddenly a light from heaven flashed around him.

4 - He fell to the ground and heard a voice saying to him, Saulo, Saulo, why are you persecuting me?

5 - Who are you, Lord? Saul asked. The Lord replied: I am Jesus, whom you persecute.

6 - Get up and go into the city, where they will tell you what to do.

7 - The men who accompanied him stopped speechless, hearing the voice, but seeing no one.

8 - Saul got up from the ground, and, opening his eyes, he could not see anything. Then, guided by the hand, he was taken to Damascus.

9 - He was three days without seeing, during which he neither ate nor drank."

In this episode, Saulo had an extraordinary personal experience when he met Jesus on the way to Damascus. This life-changing experience led to a radical change of heart and enabled him to discern the true identity of Jesus Christ.

Saulo's personal experience with Jesus illustrates how an intimate and direct encounter with God can shape our understanding and make us better able to discern the Lord's genuine guidance amidst other voices and influences.

Nicodemus' Encounter with Jesus - John 3:1-21

The story of Nicodemus' encounter with Jesus, narrated in John 3:1-21, is another striking example of the power of personal experience in the journey of discernment:

"1 - Now there was a man among the Pharisees named Nicodemus, a leader of the Jews.

2 - This one went to Jesus at night and said to him: Rabbi, we know that you are a Teacher come from God; for no one can do these signs that you do unless God is with him.

3 - Jesus answered him, Truly, truly, I say to you, unless one is born again, he cannot see the kingdom of God.

4 - Nicodemos asked him: How can a man be born, being old? Can he enter a second time into his mother's womb and be born?

5 - Jesus answered, Truly, truly, I say to you, unless one is born of water and the Spirit, he cannot enter the kingdom of God.

6 - What is born of the flesh is flesh; and that which is born of the Spirit is spirit.

7 - Do not be surprised that I said to you: it is important for you to be born again.

8-The wind blows where it wants, you hear its voice, but you don't know where it comes from, nor where it goes; so is everyone who is born of the Spirit.

9 - Nicodemus answered and said to him, How can this be?

10 - Jesus replied: You are the master of Israel and do not know these things?

11 - Verily, verily, I say unto you, We speak what we know, and testify to what we have seen; yet you do not accept our testimony.

12 - If I told you earthly things and you did not believe, how will you believe if I tell you heavenly things?

13 - Now, no one ascended to heaven, but what came down from heaven, the Son of Man.

14 - And as Moses lifted up the serpent in the wilderness, so must the Son of Man be lifted up,

15 - so that everyone who believes in him may have eternal life.

16 - For God so loved the world, that he gave his only begotten Son, that whosoever believeth in him should not perish, but have everlasting life.

17 - For God sent his Son into the world, not to judge the world, but that the world might be saved through him.

18 - Whoever believes in him is not judged; He who does not believe is judged already, because he has not believed in the name of the only begotten Son of God.

19 - This is the judgment: that light has come into the world, and men loved darkness rather than light; because their works were evil.

20 - For everyone who does evil hates the light and does not come to the light, lest his deeds be exposed.

21 - Whoever practices the truth approaches the light, so that his works may be manifested, because they were wrought in God."

In this encounter, Nicodemus seeks Jesus at night, demonstrating a personal and discreet search for the truth. Jesus' answer about the need to be born again of the Spirit reveals the importance of the personal experience of spiritual rebirth to understand the true divine message.

Through this experience, Nicodemus was led to a deeper understanding of Jesus' teachings and the importance of believing in Him to attain eternal life. Nicodemus' personal experience with Jesus shaped his understanding and discernment of truth.

The Conversion of Zacchaeus - Luke 19:1-10

The story of Zacchaeus, as told in Lucas 19:1-10, also illustrates the transforming power of personal experience in the search for discernment:

"1 - When Jesus had entered Jericho, he was passing by.

2 - Behold, a man named Zacchaeus; he was chief publican and he was rich.

3 - I was trying to see who Jesus was, but I could not, because of the crowd, because he was of small stature.

4 - So he ran ahead and climbed a sycamore tree to see him, because he was going to pass that way.

185

5 - When Jesus arrived at that place, he looked up and said to him, Zacchaeus, come down quickly, for it matters that I stay at your house today.

6 - He came down in a hurry and received him with joy.

7 - All who saw it murmured, saying that he had lodged with a sinful man.

8 - Meanwhile, Zacchaeus stood up and said to the Lord, Lord, I resolve to give half of my goods to the poor; and if I have defrauded anyone of anything, I pay back four times as much.

9-Then Jesus said to him, Today, there has been salvation in this house, for this also is a son of Abraham.

10 - For the Son of Man came to seek and to save the lost."

In this passage, Zacchaeus seeks to see Jesus with great desire and, even facing obstacles, does not give up until he has a personal encounter with Him. The encounter with Jesus transformed Zacchaeus' heart, leading him to change his life and make the decision to be fair in his actions.

Zacchaeus' personal experience with Jesus demonstrates how a direct encounter with truth can shape our understanding and discernment, enabling us to make choices that are in line with divine will.

Mary Magdalene's Encounter with the Risen One - John 20:11-18

Mary Magdalene's encounter with Jesus after His resurrection, recorded in John 20:11-18, is a moving example of the power of personal experience to discern divine truth:

11 Mary, meanwhile, stood at the entrance to the tomb, weeping. As she wept, she bent down and looked into the tomb.

12 - He saw two angels dressed in white, sitting where the body of Jesus had been, one at the head and the other at the feet.

13 - They asked her, Woman, why are you crying? He said to them, Because they have taken my Lord, and I do not know where they have put him.

14 - Having said this, he turned back and saw Jesus standing, but he did not know that it was Jesus.

15 - Jesus asked her: Woman, why are you crying? Who are you looking for? Assuming it was the gardener, she replied: Sir, if you took it away, tell me where you put it, and I will take it.

16 - Jesus said to her: Mary! She, turning around, exclaimed in Hebrew: Raboni! (which means Master).

17 - Jesus said to him, Detain me not; for I have not yet ascended to my Father, but go to my brothers and tell them that I ascend to my Father and your Father, to my God and your God.

18 - Then Mary Magdalene ran, announcing to the disciples: I have seen the Lord! And he told them what Jesus had said to him."

Mary Magdalene's personal experience with the risen Jesus was transformative and transcendent. She went from deep sadness at witnessing the empty tomb to immense joy at finding the Master alive. This intimate encounter with Jesus enabled her to discern the true reality of the resurrection and to share this news with the other disciples.

These examples highlight the importance of personal experience in seeking to discern divine revelations. Like Samuel, Nicodemus, Zacchaeus, and Mary Magdalene, each of us can have personal encounters with the Lord that shape our understanding and enable us to distinguish between true divine guidance and false discourse.

Personal experience can be a reliable compass in the maze of discernment, allowing us to develop an intimate understanding of God's word and His will for our lives. By opening our hearts to experience the divine, we become more sensitive to the voice of the Lord and better able to reject the illusions and seductions of false prophets.

THE TRAPS OF PRESUMPTION

Presumption is a dangerous snare that can lead genuine prophets astray from the path of humility and lead them to exalt themselves above the divine will. In this chapter, we will enter the universe of presumption, seeking to understand its causes and identify the subtle signs that can hide behind beautiful words. For this, we will turn to the Holy Scriptures to find teachings and examples that warn us about the dangers of presumption and guide us in the search for spiritual discernment.

The Origin of Presumption

Presumption has its roots in the pride and arrogance of the human heart. It manifests itself when someone puts himself above others, relying excessively on his own abilities and knowledge, neglecting dependence on God. This arrogant attitude can lead prophets to consider themselves the exclusive bearers of divine truth, closing themselves off from dialogue and the possibility of correction.

The Bible warns us about the danger of presumption in Proverbs 16:18: "Pride goes before ruin, and the haughtiness of the spirit before a fall." This verse teaches us that those who exalt themselves too much are destined to face disastrous consequences. Presumption blinds the heart to errors and weaknesses, making it unable to see the need for humility and submission to the will of God.

The Danger of Prophetic Presumption

Presumption can manifest itself most dangerously in those who set themselves up as prophets and messengers of God. The legitimate desire to transmit the divine word can be corrupted when the quest for recognition and prestige takes precedence over the quest to obey God's will. Prophetic presumption can lead the prophet to speak in the name of God without being truly sent by Him, resulting in empty and misleading revelations.

A biblical example that illustrates the danger of prophetic presumption is the story of the prophet Balaam, narrated in Numbers 22 to 24. Balaam was a renowned prophet, but his greed led him to give in to King Balak's temptation to curse the people of Israel in exchange for material rewards. Even though he heard God's warning, Balaam persisted in his presumptuous path, which led him to pronounce blessings upon Israel, but also to be responsible for enticing Israel to sin through idolatry and immorality (Numbers 31:16).

The Signs of Prophetic Presumption

Identifying the signs of presumption in prophets is not an easy task, as presumption is often masked by eloquence and apparent wisdom. However, the Bible offers us valuable clues for discerning presumption and its pitfalls. Some characteristics that can give away the presumption are:

Vainglory and Self-promotion

Conceit manifests itself in the desire for self-promotion and the search for recognition and praise. Presumptuous prophets tend to exalt themselves and emphasize their own accomplishments rather than giving all the credit to God. They may exaggerate their spiritual experiences to impress others, creating an inflated image of themselves.

Jesus teaches us about the importance of humility in Matthew 23:12: "Whoever exalts himself will be humbled; and whoever humbles himself will be exalted." Humility is an antidote to conceit, as it recognizes that all our abilities and gifts come from God and that we are but servants in His hands.

Unsubstantiated Revelations

One of the main signs of prophetic presumption is the proclamation of revelations that have no foundation in Scripture and the will of God. Genuine prophets speak for God, conveying His words and teachings, while presumptuous ones may be moved by their own personal fantasies and desires.

Jeremiah 23:16 warns about the prophets who "make them an empty foundation, even the vision of their own heart", that is, their visions do not come from God, but are creations of their own mind. These empty revelations can lead people to follow wrong paths and distance them from the true will of God.

lack of regret

Presumption often manifests itself in resistance to recognizing mistakes and repenting. Smug prophets can become inflexible in their positions, ignoring rebukes or corrections, which prevents them from growing spiritually and deepening their relationship with God.

The prophet Nathan was an example of humility and repentance in his interaction with King David. Upon confronting David with his sin of adultery and murder, Nathan received the king's reaction of sincere repentance (2 Samuel 12:13). This act of humility allowed David to experience God's mercy and forgiveness, demonstrating that humility and a readiness to recognize mistakes are essential characteristics of a true prophet.

The Prevention of Prejudice

To avoid falling into the pitfalls of presumption, it is essential to cultivate a life of humility and devotion to God. Some practices that can help us prevent presumption include:

Continuous Search for the Will of God

Prophets must continually seek God's will in prayer and meditation on the Scriptures. The quest to know and understand God's will must be constant and sincere, leading them to humbly submit to what He reveals.

194

Salmo 119:105 declares, "Your word is a lamp to my feet, and a light to my path." The Word of God is a light that illuminates our path and guides us towards the truth. Those who want to be true messengers of God must cling to His word, allowing it to guide them and mold their hearts.

Communion and Accountability

Fellowship with other brothers and spiritual leaders is an important way to avoid presumption. Through accountability and sharing with people who are wise and mature in the faith, prophets can receive guidance and correction, remaining humble before God and others.

Proverbs 27:17 states: "As iron as iron is sharpened, so a man sharpens the face of his friend." Communion with other brothers in the faith strengthens us and helps us to grow spiritually. The exchange of experiences and knowledge helps us to remain vigilant against the dangers of presumption.

Renouncement of the Ego

Renunciation of the ego and the pursuit of selfless service are fundamental to combating conceit. Prophets must remember that their mission is to serve God and others, not seek personal glory or recognition.

The Apostle Paul teaches us in Philippians 2:3-4: "Do nothing through strife or vainglory, but in humility each esteem others better than themselves; look not each man only to his own things, but each also to the things of others." Humility of heart allows us to value and serve others rather than seeking only our own interests.

THE STRENGTH OF THE COMMUNITY

The community of believers plays a vital role in the search for truth and in discerning divine revelations. Sharing wisdom, experiences, and knowledge among community members can protect one another from the pitfalls of presumptuous prophets, strengthening the bond that unites you as followers of the Lord. In this chapter, we will explore the importance of community in spiritual life, highlighting how the unity of the faithful can be a powerful force in identifying and correcting false revelations.

197

Community in Holy Scripture

Since biblical times, the importance of the community of believers has been emphasized in Holy Scripture. In the Law of Moses, God instructed the people of Israel to live in fellowship and care for one another. In Leviticus 19:18, the Lord commands: "Thou shalt love thy neighbor as thyself." This principle of love and mutual care lays the foundation for the formation of a strong and cohesive community.

The book of Proverbs also contains several teachings about the importance of collective wisdom. Proverbs 15:22 declares, "Projects fail for lack of counsel, but succeed when there are many counselors." This passage underscores the need to seek advice and guidance from the community in order to make wise decisions and avoid deviations.

The New Testament also emphasizes the value of Christian community. In Acts of Apostles 2:42-47, we have a picture of the life of the first Christians who dedicated themselves to the teaching of the apostles, to fellowship, to the breaking of bread and to prayers. They shared everything in common and cared for one another unselfishly, forming a united community around faith in Jesus Christ.

The Community as a Source of Wisdom

The community of believers is a rich source of wisdom and spiritual insight. Members share their personal experiences with God, their study of the Scriptures, and the revelations they have received. This exchange of knowledge can help to illuminate and enrich each individual's understanding, enabling them to discern truth from presumption.

Proverbs 11:14 underscores the importance of the wise advice given by the many advisers: "Without divine guidance the people fall, but victory is obtained with many advisers." The community of believers serves as a group of spiritual advisors who can offer different insights and perspectives, contributing to a broader and deeper view of spiritual issues.

In addition, the community provides a safe environment for the faithful to share their doubts, questions and concerns. When someone faces spiritual dilemmas, having the support and guidance of brothers in Christ can bring clarity and encouragement. The community's unity allows its members to support each other in their journeys of faith.

Discerning Together: Protecting Community

The community of believers not only shares wisdom, but also serves as a line of defense against the pitfalls of presumptuous prophets. When dubious revelations or suspected prophets arise, the community can discern together, assessing the veracity of the messages and the authenticity of the prophets.

1 John 4:1 instructs us to test the spirits to discern whether they are of God: "Beloved, believe not every spirit, but try the spirits whether they are of God: because many false prophets are gone out into the world." This spiritual test is most effective when carried out in community, where different perspectives and experiences can be shared to achieve broader insight.

The apostle Paul also exhorts Christians to discern the teachings and prophecies received. In 1 Thessalonians 5:20-21, he says, "Do not despise prophecies, but put everything to the test. Hold fast to what is good." In this sense, the community acts as a filter, retaining what is good and discarding what is false.

Communion in Adversity

The community of believers also plays an essential role in protecting and restoring those who have been deceived by false prophets. When someone is led astray by presumption, the fellowship of the community can offer support, love, and compassion during the process of repentance and restoration.

Galatians 6:1-2 highlights the importance of fellowship to help brothers and sisters carry their burdens: "Brothers, if anyone is caught doing something wrong, you who are spiritual correct him in a spirit of gentleness; The community is called to lovingly correct and help restore those who have fallen, remembering that they too are vulnerable to temptation.

The Community as a Model of Unity

The community of the faithful is called to be a model of unity and fraternal love. By demonstrating mutual care and wise discernment, community members witness to the world the true essence of the Christian faith.

Ephesians 4:3 exhorts us to "keep the unity of the Spirit in the bond of peace." Unity is essential for the community to remain strong and protected against the attacks of false prophets. Love and compassion for one another are fundamental to the spiritual growth of the community.

THE SEARCH FOR DIVINE WISDOM

Divine wisdom is a priceless treasure that illuminates the path of spiritual discernment. In the journey of faith, believers are invited to seek that wisdom, which enables them to receive authentic revelations and to discern truth among the many voices clamoring for attention. In this chapter, we will explore spiritual practices that bring believers closer to the Lord, allowing them to access divine wisdom and grow in discernment.

The Fountain of Divine Wisdom

Divine wisdom is a gift from God to those who sincerely seek Him. Proverbs 2:6 declares, "For the Lord gives wisdom, and out of his mouth come knowledge and understanding." Wisdom comes from God himself and is accessible to all who seek Him in humility and devotion.

James 1:5 it also encourages us to seek wisdom from God: "And if any of you lacks wisdom, let him ask of God, who gives to all liberally and does not rebuke, and it will be given him." This passage assures us that God is ready to grant us the wisdom needed to discern the paths of life and recognize spiritual truths.

Prayer as a Means of Communion

Prayer is one of the most powerful means of communion with God and a way to access divine wisdom. Through prayer, we can share our doubts, questions and anxieties with the Lord, seeking His guidance and wisdom.

Jesus taught us to pray in Matthew 6:9-13, in the prayer known as the Our Father. In that prayer, we recognize the greatness of God and seek His will in our lives. Through prayer, we can receive revelations from the Holy Spirit and discern truth from false promises.

Reading and Meditation on the Holy Scriptures

The Holy Scriptures are a rich source of divine wisdom. Through reading and meditating on the Word of God, believers are edified and strengthened in their faith, gaining spiritual insight.

Salmo 119:105 declares, "Your word is a lamp to my feet, and a light to my path." The Scriptures are a light that guides the way of believers, showing them truth and principles to follow. Meditating on the Scriptures allows divine wisdom to penetrate their hearts and help them to discern between right and wrong.

Hebrews 4:12 emphasizes the effectiveness of the Word of God in discerning the thoughts and intents of the heart: "For the word of God is living and active, and sharper than any two-edged sword, piercing even to the division of soul and spirit, and of joints and marrow, and is able to discern the thoughts and intentions of the heart." God's Word is a powerful tool for spiritual discernment, exposing the motives and intentions of the human heart.

Learning from Church Tradition

Church tradition is a valuable source of spiritual wisdom. Through the teachings of Church fathers and saints down through the centuries, believers can learn from the experience and wisdom of those who came before them.

Hebrews 13:7 encourages us to remember the leaders who taught us the Word of God: "Remember your shepherds, who spoke the word of God to you, whose faith imitate, paying attention to their way of living." By learning from those who maintained faith and godly wisdom, we can avoid past mistakes and grow in spiritual discernment.

The Direction of the Holy Spirit

The Holy Spirit plays a crucial role in seeking divine wisdom and discerning spiritual truths. Jesus promised to send the Holy Spirit to guide us into all truth (John 16:13), and the presence of the Holy Spirit in our lives enables us to discern among the voices that cry out for attention.

Galatians 5:22-23 tells us of the fruits of the Spirit, which include love, joy, peace, longsuffering, gentleness, goodness, faithfulness, meekness, and self-control. When we are guided by the Holy Spirit, we bear these fruits in our lives, and they help us to discern what is true and authentic among the many voices of the world.

Learning from Experience and the Life of Faith

The pursuit of godly wisdom also involves learning from the experience and lives of faith of other believers. The testimonies of people who have gone through experiences of overcoming, testing and spiritual growth can be valuable sources of teaching and discernment.

Romans 15:4 tells us, "For whatever was written in the past was written to teach us, so that through endurance and the encouragement of the Scriptures we might have hope." Through the experience recorded in the Scriptures and the stories of faith shared by the brothers, we are edified in our search for divine wisdom.

The Need for Humility

Humility is an essential virtue in the quest for divine wisdom. Recognizing our dependence on God and our limitations as human beings allows us to open our hearts to divine wisdom.

Proverbs 11:2 says: "When pride comes, dishonor comes, but with the humble is wisdom." Those who approach God in humility and reverence have their hearts open to His wisdom and insight.

Discerning Between Worldly Wisdom and Divine Wisdom

In the quest for divine wisdom, we also face the challenge of discerning between worldly wisdom and wisdom that comes from God. The wisdom of the world is often based on values and principles that conflict with God's Word, and therefore requires spiritual discernment to separate what is true from what is misleading.

1 Corinthians 1:20-21 highlights the difference between the wisdom of the world and divine wisdom: "Where is the wise man? Where is the scribe? Where is the inquirer of this age? Has not God made the wisdom of the world foolish? Since, in the wisdom of God, the world did not know him through his own wisdom, it pleased God to save those who believe through the foolishness of preaching." Divine wisdom may seem foolishness in the eyes of the world, but it is the only one that leads to true spiritual life.

Wisdom in Decision Making

The quest for divine wisdom is also closely linked to decision-making in our daily lives. Proverbs 3:5-6 guides us: "Trust in the Lord with all your heart and lean not on your own understanding. In all your ways acknowledge him, and he will make your paths straight." By trusting God and seeking His wisdom, we are guided in our decisions and avoid paths that lead to presumption and error.

The Continuous Journey of Searching for Divine Wisdom

The search for divine wisdom is an ongoing journey in the believer's life. As we grow in intimacy with God, we are graced with the wisdom needed to discern truth and avoid the pitfalls of presumption and false voices.

Through prayer, meditating on the Scriptures, learning from Church tradition, the leading of the Holy Spirit, and humility before God, we can grow in discernment and find true wisdom that lights our path.

May we continue in our quest for divine wisdom, guided by the Holy Spirit and strengthened by communion with God and the community of believers. May divine wisdom enable us to discern the truth and live in accordance with the Lord's will, avoiding the pitfalls of presumption and seeking a life of deep intimacy with God.

THE REFUGE IN UNCONDITIONAL LOVE

The Lord's unconditional love is a safe haven for sincere hearts. In this chapter, we will understand how divine love sustains believers through the trials of discernment, giving them confidence to face uncertainty and courage to reject presumptuous speech.

God's Love in Creation

God's unconditional love has been evident since the creation of the world. Genesis 1 relates how God created all things through His mighty love and wisdom. With each creative act, God beheld His work and saw that it was good. This loving care for creation also extends to human beings, created in His image and likeness. (Genesis 1:27). God's love is so deep that He has given us free will, allowing us to choose to know Him and love Him in return.

God's Unconditional Love in the History of the People of Israel

The history of the people of Israel is marked by God's unconditional love, despite the people's constant failures and infidelities. The book of Exodus relates how God delivered the people of Israel from slavery in Egypt, leading them safely through the Red Sea and guiding them in the wilderness for forty years. This caring love is illustrated through divine providence, such as the manna that fell from heaven to sustain the people during their wilderness journey. (Exodus 16).

In Isaiah 43:1, God declares, "Fear not, for I have redeemed you; I have called you by your name, you are mine." These words

210

reveal God's unconditional love for His people, showing that He knows them individually and is always there to protect them.

The Love of God Revealed in Jesus Christ

The apex of God's unconditional love is revealed in Jesus Christ, His beloved Son, sent into the world to redeem humanity from sin. John 3:16 is a widely known passage that expresses this unconditional love: "For God so loved the world, that he gave his only begotten Son, that whosoever believeth in him should not perish, but have everlasting life."

The life, death and resurrection of Jesus are the ultimate proof of God's love for us. He sacrificed His beloved Son so that we could be reconciled to Him and receive salvation through faith in Jesus.

Unconditional Love and Spiritual Discernment

God's unconditional love is an essential element in spiritual discernment. When we seek to hear the voice of God amidst the diverse voices of the world, knowledge of His love enables us to distinguish between the genuine word of the Lord and presumptuous illusions.

In Ephesians 3:17-19, the apostle Paul expresses his prayer that believers would be rooted and grounded in the love of Christ:

"That Christ may dwell in your hearts through faith; that, being rooted and grounded in love, you may be able to comprehend with all the saints what is the breadth and length and height and depth, and to know the love of Christ, which surpasses knowledge, that you may be filled with all the fullness of God."

Knowing and experiencing God's unconditional love makes us more sensitive to His voice, allowing us to discern the true motivation behind the words of prophets and preachers. Divine love also gives us courage to reject empty and presumptuous words that do not come from the Lord.

Unconditional Love as a Refuge in Trials

Spiritual discernment can be a challenge amid life's trials and adversity. God's unconditional love reveals itself as a safe haven in times of uncertainty and confusion.

In Romans 8:38-39, Paul assures believers: "For I am persuaded, that neither death, nor life, nor angels, nor principalities, nor powers, nor things present, nor things to come, nor height, nor depth, nor any other created thing, shall be able to separate us from the love of God, which is in Christ Jesus our Lord." These words are a reminder that no matter what happens, God's love remains steadfast, a safe haven for believers in all circumstances.

Unconditional Love and Trust in Discernment

When we rely on God's unconditional love, our confidence in spiritual discernment is strengthened. Knowing that we are loved by a faithful and caring God, we can face the difficulties of discernment with hope and certainty that He will guide our steps.

Proverbs 3:5-6 reminds us, "Trust in the Lord with all your heart and lean not on your own understanding. In all your ways acknowledge him, and he will make your paths straight." Confidence in God's love helps us to entrust our decisions and insights to Him, knowing that He will make our paths straight according to His will.

Unconditional Love and Rejection of Presumptuous Words

Presumption and vanity can lead prophets and preachers to offer words that do not come from God. God's unconditional love gives us the courage and firmness to reject these words and seek only the true word of the Lord.

In Jeremiah 23:16, God warns of prophets who "cause my people to err by their lies and their levity." Through the discernment provided by divine love, we can identify these false words and reject them, seeking true guidance from the Lord.

213

Unconditional Love and the Capacity to Love Others

God's unconditional love also enables us to genuinely and compassionately love others. When we understand the love God has for us, we are inspired to extend that love to others by seeking to discern their needs and offering support and care on their spiritual journeys.

1 John 4:7-8 teaches us: "Beloved, let us love one another; for love is from God; and whoever loves is born of God and knows God. He who does not love does not know God; for God is love." God's unconditional love is the source of our love for others, which helps us to walk together in search of truth and discernment.

Unconditional Love as a Lighthouse in the Midst of Doubts

In our journey of discernment, we may come across doubts and questions. God's unconditional love is like a lighthouse that guides and guides us through uncertainties.

In 1 John 4:18, we read: "There is no fear in love; rather, perfect love casts out fear. Now fear brings torment; therefore, he who fears is not perfected in love." When we understand God's perfect love, our fears and uncertainties are dispelled, allowing us to discern with clarity and certainty.

Living in God's Unconditional Love

Living in God's unconditional love is a life-changing experience. This love shapes, empowers, and sustains us along our journey of faith and discernment.

Ephesians 3:17-19 teaches us that when we are rooted and grounded in the love of Christ, we can comprehend His greatness and be filled with all the fullness of God. This fullness enables us to discern the truth, reject presumptuous words, and live in deep intimacy with God.

May we embrace God's unconditional love in our hearts, allowing it to guide, strengthen and empower us in our quest for spiritual discernment. May divine love be our safe refuge amidst trials, giving us confidence to meet the challenges of discernment with hope and courage. And, above all, may this love inspire us to love others and seek the Lord's true guidance in all areas of our lives.

THE VICTORY OF THE TRUTH

In this inspiring chapter, we will witness the victory of truth over presumption. Sincere prophets who embraced humility and discerned the divine word became beacons of hope and inspiration for their communities, guiding them closer to the heart of the Lord.

The prophet Elijah is a notable figure in the history of the people of Israel. His ministry was marked by courage, boldness and faithfulness to the word of the Lord. In the first book of Kings, chapter 18, we find the account of one of the most memorable moments in Elijah's life: the confrontation with the prophets of Baal on Mount Carmel.

In this episode, Elijah faced the presumption of the false prophets of Baal and the god Asherah, who led the worship of pagan gods in Israel. He challenged them to offer a sacrifice to their god, while he himself would offer one to the Lord. The true God would respond by fire consuming the sacrifice.

Despite the apparent numerical disadvantage, with 450 prophets of Baal against Elijah, he did not waver. With humility and trust in the Lord, he prepared the altar, watered it with water three times, and when the time for prayer came, God answered with fire from heaven, consuming Elijah's sacrifice. This powerful event led the people to recognize the true divinity of the Lord and to turn to Him again. (1 Kings 18:37-39).

Elijah's story teaches us the importance of standing firm in the truth, even in the midst of presumption and idolatry. Your courage and faith in the Lord show that the victory of truth will prevail over falsehood.

Daniel: Firmness in Faith

Another notable prophet is Daniel, whose life is narrated in the book of the same name. During the Babylonian exile, he and his friends faced pressure to worship the pagan gods of the empire, but they refused to budge.

In Daniel 1, we see that Daniel and his friends were taken to King Nebuchadnezzar's palace, where they were to be trained to serve the king. However, they refused to defile themselves with the king's food, as this would violate the dietary laws of their faith in God. With humility and respect, they asked to be fed only vegetables and water.

God blessed their obedience, and they turned out to be healthier and wiser than the other young men who submitted to the royal diet. This experience highlighted the faithfulness of Daniel and his friends to the Lord and showed that true worship cannot be compromised by presumption or cultural pressure.

In Daniel 3, another notable moment of steadfastness in faith is recorded when King Nebuchadnezzar ordered everyone to worship the statue he had erected. However, Sadrac, Meshach and Abednego refused to worship any deity other than the true God.

Despite the threat of being thrown into the fiery furnace, they remained steadfast in their faith. God miraculously delivered them from the fire, demonstrating once again that truth triumphs over presumption and idolatry.

John the Baptist: The Humble Forerunner

In the New Testament narrative, we find John the Baptist, the forerunner of Jesus Christ. He preached the arrival of the Kingdom of God and the need to repent of sins. His fervent preaching and humility made it clear that his mission was not to promote himself, but to point to the One who was to come.

In Matthew 3:11, John declares, "I baptize you with water unto repentance: but he that cometh after me is mightier than I, whose shoes I am not worthy to bear: he shall baptize you with the Holy Ghost, and with fire."

This humble statement reflects the true nature of an authentic prophet, who recognizes his insignificance in the face of the greatness of the Lord. John the Baptist did not seek personal glory, but prepared the way for the Messiah, showing that humility is a fundamental virtue for those who wish to discern and share the truth.

Pedro: Transformation through Love

The apostle Peter is a powerful example of how love and repentance can transform a presumptuous heart into a heart filled with humility and genuine love for God.

In Matthew 16:21-23, we see Peter oppose Jesus when He spoke about His future death and resurrection. Peter assumed he knew what was best for Jesus and tried to dissuade him from following God's plan. However, Jesus rebuked him, showing that Peter was thinking about human things and not the things of God.

However, Peter's experience of repentance came after Jesus' betrayal. He denied knowing the Master three times, despite pledging absolute loyalty. The pangs of remorse brought Peter to true repentance, and his humility was manifested when he threw himself at Jesus' feet and acknowledged Him as Lord. (Lucas 22:61-62).

Through this experience, Peter learned the importance of abandoning presumption and trusting God completely. He became a transformed leader, dedicated to spreading the truth and love of Christ. His story illustrates how humility and repentance can shape and enable a heart to discern and follow the Lord's truth.

Paul: From Persecutor to Humble Preacher

Another impactful story of transformation is that of Paul, initially known as Saul of Tarsus. Before his conversion, Paul was a ferocious persecutor of Christians, fueled by the presumption that he was serving God by eliminating the followers of Jesus.

However, in Acts 9, we find the account of Paul's dramatic conversion on the road to Damascus. He had a personal encounter with the risen Jesus Christ, who confronted him with the truth of his actions. This encounter left him temporarily blind and caused him to question everything he believed to be true.

After this life-changing encounter, Paul experienced true repentance and humility. He went on to be one of the greatest preachers of the Gospel, dedicated to spreading God's true message. His journey from presumption to humility is a powerful example of how God's truth can prevail, transforming hearts and directing them to true worship.

Mary: Exemplary Humility

In this chapter on the victory of truth over presumption, we cannot fail to mention Mary, the mother of Jesus. Mary was chosen by God to be the mother of the Savior and she fulfilled this mission with humility and submission to the divine will.

In the book of Luke, we find Mary's song known as the Magnificat, (Lucas 1:46-55), in which she exalts the greatness of God and recognizes her own smallness before Him. She humbly submits to God's will, proclaiming, "Behold, I am the handmaid of the Lord; be it to me according to your word." (Lucas 1:38).

Mary's humility is an example of how truth prevails when a heart surrenders completely to the will of God. Her dedication to true worship and fulfilling the divine plan made her a powerful figure in salvation history.

The Victory of Truth Today

The victory of truth over presumption is not limited to antiquity; it is a perennial principle that extends to the present day. Many spiritual and faithful leaders around the world testify how the truth of the Gospel has triumphed in their lives and communities.

In Christian churches and communities, we see examples of modern prophets who, with humility and devotion, discern the divine word and share it with their brothers and sisters in Christ. They are leaders who seek the truth with integrity, promoting unity and mutual love among the faithful.

Furthermore, the victory of truth can be witnessed in individuals who, in the face of transformative experiences, rediscover their true faith and become beacons of hope in their communities. They are testimonies of people who abandoned their presumptions and surrendered to God's unconditional love, becoming instruments of true worship.

THE JOURNEY OF SPIRITUAL MATURITY

In the final chapter of this third part, we will understand that discernment is an ongoing journey of spiritual growth. By embracing the Lord's wisdom and cultivating a humble heart, believers will be prepared to face life's challenges and discern the true word that comes from the Lord, without fearing presumptuous prophets.

The Path of Wisdom

The search for spiritual maturity begins with the search for divine wisdom. In Proverbs 2:6, we find the promise that the Lord is the source of wisdom and the knower of all that is right. Wisdom is an essential quality for discerning between truth and presumption.

The book of Proverbs is filled with teachings about wisdom and the need to seek it diligently. In Proverbs 4:7, we read: "Wisdom is the main thing; therefore get wisdom; yes, with all that thou hast get understanding." This call to seek wisdom shows that it is an ongoing endeavor and that we must be willing to learn and grow in our knowledge of the Lord.

Humility as a Pillar of Spiritual Maturity

Throughout this book, we have seen how humility is a fundamental virtue in the journey of discernment. Humility allows us to recognize that we are not the holders of all truth and that our understanding is subject to limitations. As we embrace humility, we are open to hearing God's voice and receiving His revelations with a gentle heart.

In James 4:10, we are exhorted to humble ourselves before the Lord, and He will exalt us. This promise shows that humility is not a sign of weakness, but a path to divine exaltation. When we recognize our dependence on God and submit ourselves to Him, we are enabled to discern truth and resist presumption.

Growing in the Word of God

God's Word is a light to our path (Salmo 119:105) and a source of wisdom and insight. As we delve deeper into the Scriptures, we cultivate a deeper knowledge of God's will and are enabled to discern the true word that comes from Him.

In Hebrews 5:12-14, we are exhorted to become masters of the Word of God, able to discern between good and evil. This highlights the importance of growing in our understanding of the Scriptures and applying their teachings in our daily lives.

The Combat of Presumption

Presumption is a dangerous snare that can lead believers astray from the path of truth. To combat conceit, we need to be alert to the signs of pride and arrogance in our hearts. The apostle Paul warns us in Romans 12:3: "For by the grace given to me, I say to each one of you not to think of yourself more highly than you ought, but rather to think in moderation, according to the measure of faith which God has apportioned to each one."

Moderation and humility are antidotes to presumption. When we recognize our own limitations and trust God to guide us, we are less likely to fall into the trap of conceit.

The Power of Prayer

Prayer is a powerful tool on the journey to spiritual maturity. Through prayer, we connect with God and seek His wisdom and insight. In Philippians 4:6-7, we are encouraged to present our petitions to God with thanksgiving, and the peace of God will guard our hearts and minds in Christ Jesus.

Prayer allows us to surrender our worries and anxieties to God, seeking His guidance and direction in our decisions and discernment. When we pray with a sincere and humble heart, God answers us, and we are enabled to discern the truth amid the circumstances of life.

The Journey of Spiritual Maturity

The journey of spiritual maturity is one of continuous learning, growth and transformation. As we embrace the Lord's wisdom, cultivate humility in our hearts, and delve deeper into God's Word, we are prepared to face life's challenges with discernment and confidence in the truth.

Like the examples of prophets and believers throughout history, we can be beacons of hope and inspiration for our communities, guiding them to true worship and helping them discern the Lord's genuine word.

THE BALLOON ASCENSION

In this chapter, we will learn about the trajectory of Balão, a false prophet whose prophecies were tinged with greed and the desire for personal enrichment. Through his seductive words, Balão conquered followers eager to hear his promises, without realizing the darkness that was hidden behind his apparent divine revelations.

229

Introduction to Balloon

In the book of Numbers, we find the story of Balloon, a character who became known for his misleading prophecies and his pursuit of personal gain. The narrative begins with the fear of the inhabitants of Moab before the people of Israel, who were approaching their land. The king of Moab, Balak, summoned Balam, a pagan prophet, to curse Israel and drive them away from their lands. (Numbers 22:2-6).

Although Balloon was a prophet, his motives were questionable from the start. He was more interested in the riches and rewards offered by Balak than in hearing God's voice. This greed and ambition distorted his revelations and led him to prophesy things that did not come from the Lord.

The Deceptive Appearances

Balloon knew that the Lord God had blessed Israel and that he could not curse them. However, he gave in to the temptation of money and a prominent position offered by Balak. On the way to curse the people of Israel, Balloon met an angel of the Lord who opposed him. The angel of God was there to prevent Balloon from following his sinful mission. (Numbers 22:22-35).

But instead of repenting for his bad intentions, Balão continued, convinced that he could manipulate the situation and achieve his selfish goals. He even set up an altar and offered sacrifices to the Lord, seeking His approval to curse Israel. (Numbers 23:1-4). However, God was not deceived by Balam's hypocrisy and, instead of cursing, he ended up blessing the people of Israel by order of the Lord.

The Dissonance Between Words and Actions

Balloon's story shows us the dissonance between his apparently pious words and his selfish actions. He continued to pronounce blessings on Israel even though his heart was bent on cursing them for money. This dissonance between what he said and what he really intended revealed the false nature of his prophecies.

This dissonance is a lesson for believers today. We must always examine our own motives and intentions, ensuring that our words and actions are in harmony with the truth and God's will. Hypocrisy can be subtle and dangerous, and it leads us astray from the path of true worship.

The Example of Balaam

The apostle Peter, in the New Testament, warns about the example of Balaam as a false prophet motivated by greed (2

Pedro 2:15). He describes Balaam as a man who loved the wages of injustice, that is, someone who was willing to do evil for material rewards. This is a warning for Christians to remain firm in their faith and not allow themselves to be seduced by the temptations of greed and the pursuit of material riches.

The Balloon Fall

Balão's greed and presumption eventually led to his downfall. At the end of the story, we find Balam advising Balak to seduce the Israelites into sinning so that God will be angry with them and punish them. This was Balloon's last attempt to weaken Israel and reap its selfish rewards.(Numbers 31:16).

However, his downfall was inevitable. Balam's evil plan backfired, and he was eventually killed when the Israelites defeated the Midianites, including Balak, in battle.(Numbers 31:8).

Lessons Learned

Balloon's story is a powerful reminder that discernment is essential to distinguish between genuine divine revelations and false prophecies tinged with greed and presumption. Money and the search for recognition should not influence our words and actions, as the search for truth should be our greatest motivation.

232

Furthermore, Balloon shows us that appearances can be deceiving. Even if someone utters seemingly pious words, their true intentions and motives may be unclear. We must always examine people's actions and fruits, looking for consistency between what they say and what they do.

Balão's example is a warning for the faithful to remain firm in their faith, resisting the temptations of greed and the search for material rewards. We must seek to please God above all else and allow His truth and wisdom to guide our words and actions.

In chapter 1, we explore the trajectory of Balão, a false prophet who was motivated by greed and the pursuit of personal gain. His prophecies were tinged with the darkness of his intentions, and he sought to curse the people of Israel in exchange for material rewards. Balão's story serves as a powerful wake-up call for believers, reminding us of the importance of discernment, humility and the pursuit of true worship of God, above any greed or personal ambition.

THE SUBTLE DISTINCTION

The difference between an authentic prophet and a false prophet is not always obvious. In this chapter, we will explore the subtle distinction between those who genuinely seek God's will and those who use spirituality as a means to further their own interests.

234

The Essence of Authentic Prophecy

True prophetism is a divine calling aimed at conveying God's messages to His people. Authentic prophets are God's instruments, chosen to proclaim His word, direct His people, and call to conversion those who have strayed from the path of righteousness.

A classic example of an authentic prophet is Moses. He was chosen by God to lead the Israelites and guide them towards the Promised Land. In Deuteronomy 34:10, the Bible states that there never again appeared in Israel another prophet like Moses, who knew the Lord face to face. Moses did not seek to be a prophet for his own interests; he fulfilled his mission out of love and obedience to God.

False Prophets and Their Dark Intentions

On the other hand, false prophets are motivated by selfish interests such as power, fame and wealth. They use spirituality as a means to achieve their personal goals and deceive those around them. Instead of seeking God's will, they create false revelations to impress and manipulate others.

In Jeremiah 23:21-22, we find a warning about false prophets who dare to prophesy in God's name, even without having

235

received any message from Him: "I did not send these prophets, but they ran;

The Test of Time

One way to discern between true and false prophets is the test of time. The true prophecies of God are undeniably fulfilled, while the false ones fade and do not come true. In Deuteronomy 18:21-22, God gives a clear guideline: "Perhaps you say to each other, 'How do we know if the message is not from the Lord?' If what the prophet proclaims in the name of the Lord does not come to pass or come to pass, that message is not from the Lord. That prophet spoke presumptuously. Do not be afraid of him."

The Example of Hananiah

In the book of Jeremiah, we find the example of Hananiah, a false prophet who prophesied falsely to the people of Israel. He claimed that in just two years, the Lord would restore everything that had been taken from the temple, including the sacred vessels that had been taken to Babylon. (Jeremiah 28:2-4).

However, the prophet Jeremiah, a true messenger of God, confronted Hananiah and warned him of the consequences of his false prophecies. Jeremiah made it clear that the fulfillment of prophecy would depend on aligning with God's will and that falsely prophesying would only lead to disgrace. (Jeremiah 28:5-9).

The Motivation Behind the Words

The subtle distinction between the authentic prophet and the false prophet also lies in the motivation behind the proclaimed words. While the genuine prophet seeks to glorify God and serve His people, the false prophet seeks his own interests, using spirituality as a vehicle to achieve his selfish goals.

Jesus warned about false prophets in Matthew 7:15, saying, "Beware of false prophets. They come to you in sheep's clothing, but inwardly they are ravening wolves." Here, Jesus emphasizes the importance of discerning the dark intentions that can hide behind godly appearances.

The Quest for Personal Glory

One of the main signs of a false prophet is the pursuit of personal glory and recognition. They want to be admired and idolized by others. However, the true prophet puts God at the center of everything and seeks only His will and glory.

In John 7:18, Jesus stated, "He who speaks on his own seeks his own glory; but he who seeks the glory of him who sent him, this one is true, and no injustice is in him."

The Role of the Community

The community of believers plays a crucial role in identifying false prophets. By sharing wisdom and insight, community members can protect each other from the snares of presumptuous prophets, strengthening the bond that unites them as followers of the Lord.

In 1 John 4:1, the apostle John exhorts us: "Beloved, do not believe every spirit, but test the spirits to see whether they are of God, because many false prophets have gone out into the world." This guidance highlights the importance of the community in discerning the authenticity of the revelations and words spoken.

The Quest for Discernment

Discernment is an essential virtue in every person's journey of faith. It allows believers to identify the true word of God and reject the illusions of presumption. Seeking divine wisdom and cultivating an intimate connection with God are fundamental steps in developing the ability to discern between what is authentic and what is false.

In Proverbs 2:3-5, we read: "If you cry out for discernment and shout aloud for understanding, if you seek wisdom as one seeks silver and search for it as one seeks for hidden treasure, then you will understand what it is to fear the Lord and find the knowledge of God."

Humility as Protection

Humility is a powerful protection against the snares of false prophets. A humble heart is willing to recognize its own limitations and depend on divine wisdom. The quest for personal recognition is replaced by the desire to please God and obey His will.

In Proverbs 11:2, it is written: "When pride comes, then disaster comes, but wisdom is with the humble." Humility keeps us from falling into the trap of presumption and helps us to clearly discern the motivations behind the words of the prophets.

So, as we seek to develop discernment in our walk of faith, we must remember the example of Moses, who was chosen by God to be a true prophet. Through his obedience and humility, he served the people of Israel and faithfully conveyed divine messages. May we also be instruments of the Lord, transmitting His truth with sincerity and love, moving away from the traps of false prophets and getting closer and closer to the heart of God.

THE EVIL PROPHECIES

The figure of Balão, a false prophet, is a powerful example of the damage caused by obscure and manipulative revelations. His prophecies seemed to materialize, deceiving many around him and leading unsuspecting hearts into crooked paths. In this chapter, we will delve into Balão's story, examining his actions and the dire consequences of his words, as well as reflecting on the discernment needed to identify false prophecies.

The Contextualization of Balloon

Balloon's story is found in the Old Testament, more specifically in the books of Numbers and Joshua. Balloon was a pagan soothsayer or prophet known for his cursing and blessing skills. He was invited by King Balak of Moab to curse the people of Israel, who were approaching his land.

The Balloon Dilemma

When Balloon was approached by Balak, he consulted with God about what to do. Although God initially instructed Balam not to go and curse the people of Israel, Balam insisted on going with Balak, perhaps motivated by his greed and desire for material rewards. God eventually allowed Balloon to go, but on the condition that he would speak only what God commanded him. (Numbers 22:20).

The Manipulating Prophecies

Balão's journey to meet Balak is marked by curious and even supernatural events. On the way, he was stopped by an angel with a sword, visible only to his donkey, who prevented him from continuing forward. The donkey's attitude even surprised Balão and led him to a moment of reflection.

When Balloon finally reached King Balak, he took him to high places where he could see the camp of the Israelites. Balloon then uttered his words, but despite his attempts to curse the people of Israel, only blessings came out of his mouth. This happened three times, and Balak's frustration grew as Balloon continued to bless the people he was supposed to curse.

The Curse of Balloon

Frustrated with Balam's failure to curse the Israelites, Balak sent him from his land without the reward he had promised. However, Balão, apparently unhappy with the outcome, decided to take measures to satisfy his own interests.

Balloon then gave King Balak evil advice. He suggested that Moabite women seduce the men of Israel into idolatry and sexual immorality. By corrupting the people of Israel, Balam knew that God would be angry with them, and they would be subject to His punishment. This, in turn, would allow the Moabites to defeat them in battle.

In Numbers 31:16, we can read of the consequence of Balam's manipulative words: "It was these who followed Balaam's advice, inducing the Israelites to revolt against the Lord in the incident of Peor, and a plague fell on the commonwealth of the Lord."

The Power of Greed

Balloon's behavior is a vivid example of the negative influence of greed and the desire for personal enrichment. He was willing to use his prophecy abilities to manipulate situations and people to suit his own interests. His covetousness led him to betray God's trust and act against His will.

In 2 Pedro 2:15, reference is made to Balam as a negative example: "They turned from the straight path and went to follow the way of Balaam, son of Beor, who loved the wages of injustice".

The Warning Against False Prophets

Balão's story serves as an important warning against false prophets who use spirituality as a means of seeking personal gain. The Bible is full of warnings about such people and their manipulative practices.

In Matthew 7:15, Jesus warns his disciples: "Beware of false prophets. They come to you in sheep's clothing, but inwardly they are ravening wolves."

The Distinction Between True and False Prophets

The difference between a true prophet and a false one is not always clear and evident. However, the motivation behind the

243

spoken words and alignment with God's will are crucial factors in making this distinction.

A true prophet sincerely seeks God's will and puts God's interests above his own personal interests. He speaks the truth, even when it is difficult or unpopular, and he is not corrupted by greed or covetousness.

On the other hand, a false prophet may use spirituality as a disguise to achieve his selfish goals. He may speak words that please his hearers and promise blessings and prosperity, but his intentions are obscure and aimed only at his own benefit.

The Necessary Discernment

Faced with the subtlety of distinguishing between true and false prophets, discernment is an essential virtue. Seeking divine wisdom and cultivating an intimate connection with God are key to developing this ability to discern between what is authentic and what is false.

The apostle John, in his first letter, makes an appeal for discernment: "Beloved, do not believe every spirit, but test the spirits to see whether they are from God, because many false prophets have gone out into the world." (1 John 4:1)

Greed can lead false prophets to manipulate people, using spirituality for their own ends. On the other hand, a true prophet is one who seeks God's will, putting divine interests above all else and speaking the truth with love and humility.

THE WEAKNESS OF THE SOUL

The weakness of the soul is a fertile ground where false prophets find space to sow their seeds of deceit and delusion. In this chapter, we will explore the human weaknesses that make people susceptible to the deceitful words of false prophets. We will examine how strengthening our connection with God can protect us from the pitfalls of falsehood and enable us to discern truth from lies.

246

The Human Vulnerability

Human nature is permeated with emotional and spiritual vulnerabilities. The human being is susceptible to doubts, fears, uncertainties and personal desires. These weaknesses are exploited by false prophets, who use manipulative tactics to attract followers and gain power and influence over them.

the book of Ephesians 4:14 warns of the importance of not being "carried about with every wind of doctrine, by the craftiness of men, who by cunning craftiness deceive deceitfully". This passage underscores the need to be on guard against the manipulative strategies of false prophets.

The Desire for Answers

One of the most common human weaknesses is the desire to find answers to life's complex and difficult questions. False prophets prey on this search for guidance and hope by offering simplistic solutions and empty promises that seem to respond to the emotional needs of believers.

In 2 Timothy 4:3-4, we are warned of people's tendency to seek teachers who "satisfy their own desires and accumulate for themselves teachers according to their own passions; and they will turn away from the truth and give heed to myths."

247

The Fear of the Unknown

Fear of the unknown is another weakness that can lead people to look to false prophets for answers. Uncertainties about the future, life after death and other spiritual aspects can generate anxiety and vulnerability, making them easy prey for the promises of security and protection offered by false prophets.

In the story of Jeremiah, we find an example of how fear can lead people to look for false hope. In Jeremiah 14:14, the prophet denounces the false prophets who said: "There will be no sword or famine in this place; rather, I will give you true peace".

The Need to Belong

The need to belong is an inherent characteristic of human nature. People seek out communities where they feel accepted and loved. False prophets exploit this need by creating closed groups and manipulating the loyalty of their followers to strengthen their power over them.

In Matthew 24:24, Jesus warns us about false prophets and says: "For false Christs and false prophets will arise, and they will show great signs and wonders, so as to mislead, if possible, even the elect."

248

The Power of Persuasion

False prophets are often endowed with persuasive and rhetorical skills, which make them convincing in their preaching. They know how to manipulate people's emotions and beliefs to achieve their goals. Persuasion is a powerful tool that can lead people to accept false doctrines without question.

Paul warns us about the craftiness of false prophets in Ephesians 4:14, as mentioned earlier, and in Colossians 2:4, he warns: "Lest anyone deceive you with persuasive words".

Strengthening the Connection with God

In the face of these human weaknesses, it is crucial to strengthen our connection with God to resist the wiles of false prophets. Deepening our faith, seeking an intimate relationship with God through prayer and the study of the Scriptures is essential to strengthen our spiritual foundation.

In John 10:27, Jesus reminds us: "My sheep listen to my voice; I know them, and they follow me". This intimate relationship with the Lord allows us to discern his voice from the false promises of misleading prophets.

The Quest for Biblical Knowledge

Knowledge of the Scriptures is a powerful tool for discerning truth from lies. We should diligently study God's Word and meditate on its teachings to strengthen our understanding of the truth and be on our guard against false doctrines.

In 2 Timothy 2:15, Paul advises Timothy: "Do your best to present yourself to God as one approved, a workman who does not need to be ashamed and who correctly handles the word of truth."

The Quest for Wise Counseling

Seeking wise advice from spiritual leaders, pastors and spiritual guides is a fundamental practice to avoid falling into the traps of falsehood. Experienced spiritual leaders can provide guidance and insight to help believers understand God's true message.

Proverbs 11:14 reminds us: "Where there is no advice, plans are in vain, but with the multitude of advisers, they are confirmed".

The Cultivation of Humility

Humility is an essential virtue for resisting the temptations of ego and presumption. As we cultivate humility in our hearts, we recognize our dependence on God and are less likely to give in

250

to the seduction of false prophets who seek to exalt themselves to the detriment of the truth.

In Proverbs 22:4, we read: "The reward of humility and the fear of the Lord is wealth, honor and life".

The Importance of Community

The community of believers plays a crucial role in protecting against false prophets. When we come together in community, we share wisdom, insight, and mutual support, making us stronger against the manipulative influences of false prophets.

Hebrews 10:25 encourages us "not to give up meeting together, as some are in the habit of doing, but to encourage others, and all the more as you see the Day approaching."

The Ongoing Quest for Discernment

The journey of discernment is an ongoing one, and we must always be on our guard against the deceptive tactics of false prophets. As we strengthen our connection with God, cultivate humility, and seek knowledge of the Scriptures, we will be better equipped to discern truth from lies.

Romans 12:2 exhorts us: "Do not be conformed to the pattern of this world, but be transformed by the renewing of your mind.

Then you will be able to test and approve what God desires: what is good, pleasant and perfect".

The search for answers, the fear of the unknown, the need to belong and the power of persuasion are some of the weaknesses exploited by false prophets. However, we highlight the importance of strengthening our connection with God, cultivating humility and seeking knowledge of the Scriptures to resist the wiles of falsehood.

THE PURPOSE OF
WEAKNESSES

Human weaknesses have been a constant reality throughout human history. Since the earliest times, human nature has been permeated with imperfections, failures and disappointments. And, although it may seem paradoxical, God often uses these weaknesses as instruments of spiritual growth and discernment between truth and lies.

253

Throughout the Holy Scriptures, we find several passages that deal with human weaknesses and how God acts through them to teach valuable lessons to His people. In this chapter, we will delve into these passages and understand the purpose of weaknesses in our journey of faith.

Moses' Weakness and God's Will

One of the most striking examples of how God uses human weaknesses to fulfill His purpose is recorded in the Old Testament, in the life of Moses. Moses, although he was a great leader and prophet, had his own weakness: he stuttered and had difficulties with public speaking.

When God appeared to Moses at the burning bush and called him to lead the people of Israel out of Egypt, Moses resisted. He argued that he was not eloquent and would not be able to adequately convey God's message to Pharaoh and the people. (Exodus 4:10).

Yet God answered Moses, "Who gave man a mouth? Or who makes man mute, or deaf, or sighted, or blind? Am I not the Lord?" (Exodus 4:11). God recognized Moses' weakness, but also showed him that, despite this, He would enable Moses to fulfill the mission entrusted to him.

This story teaches us that even in our weaknesses and limitations, God can empower us and use us for His purposes. When we recognize our dependence on the Lord and trust in His strength, He can accomplish great things through us.

Peter's Weakness and Christ's Redeeming Grace

In the New Testament we find the striking example of Peter's weakness. Peter was one of Jesus' closest disciples and often showed zeal and courage in following the Master. However, he also showed weakness at crucial moments.

During the Last Supper, Jesus prophesied that all of His disciples would abandon Him at the time of the Crucifixion. Peter, full of self-confidence, declared that he would never abandon Jesus, even if everyone else did.(Matthew 26:33).

But, as Jesus had predicted, when the time for the crucifixion came, Peter denied knowing Jesus three times. He gave in to pressure and fear, revealing his weakness and lack of confidence in his own words.

However, Peter's story does not end there. After Jesus' resurrection, the Lord revealed Himself again to His disciples and, in particular, to Peter. Jesus restored him by asking him three times if he loved him and, upon hearing Peter's affirmative answer, entrusted him with the task of feeding His sheep. (John 21:15-17).

Peter's weakness was no reason to disqualify him as a disciple of Jesus. On the contrary, Christ's redeeming grace was able to turn Peter's weakness into strength. The Lord used that experience of failure to teach Peter about the importance of humility, repentance, and trust in His grace and forgiveness.

Paul's Weakness and God's Power

Paul, one of the most prominent and influential apostles of early Christianity, also faced his own weaknesses. He was a man of keen intellect but, before his conversion, he fiercely persecuted and persecuted the followers of Jesus, believing that he was serving God in so doing.

However, on the road to Damascus, Paul had a life-changing encounter with the risen Jesus Christ himself. That encounter radically changed his life, and Paul became an ardent follower of Christ and a tireless apostle in the spread of the Gospel.

Even so, Paul was not without weaknesses. In his letters, he talks about a "thorn in the flesh" that afflicted him. (2 Corinthians 12:7). Although we don't know exactly what this "thorn" was, this personal weakness led him to seek God in prayer, begging Him to remove it.

256

God's response to Paul was profound and meaningful: "My grace is sufficient for you, for power is made perfect in weakness."(2 Corinthians 12:9). God showed Paul that His grace is sufficient to supply our weaknesses and that it is in recognizing our dependence on Him that we find strength.

These experiences of Moses, Peter and Paul teach us that human weaknesses are not a reason for despair or defeat, but can become opportunities for the manifestation of God's grace, power and wisdom. When we recognize our weaknesses, we are led to seek God in prayer, depend on Him and learn important lessons about trust, humility and submission to His will.

Weakness as Humility

The Bible often associates human weakness with humility. Humility is a virtue valued by God and a key element in the journey of spiritual growth and discernment between truth and lies.

In Proverbs 11:2, we read: "When pride comes, then comes dishonor, but with the humble is wisdom." This verse highlights that humility is associated with wisdom, as the humble are those who recognize their weaknesses and depend on the Lord for wisdom and discernment.

In addition, in Matthew 5:3, Jesus proclaims: "Blessed are the poor in spirit, for theirs is the Kingdom of Heaven". This "poverty of spirit" refers to humility, an awareness of our dependence on God, and an absence of arrogance and pride. Those who see themselves as weak and in need of God are blessed by Him and find true wisdom that comes from above.

Human weakness can also be a reminder of our continuing need to repent and seek God's face. In 2 Chronicles 7:14, God says, "If my people, who are called by my name, will humble themselves, and pray, and seek my face, and turn from their wicked ways, then will I hear from heaven, and will forgive their sin, and will heal their land." In this passage, God links forgiveness and healing with humility and repentance. Acknowledging our weaknesses and sins leads us to humble ourselves before God in prayer and seeking forgiveness and restoration.

The Purpose of Weaknesses in Our Judgment

Human weakness can be a powerful tool for our discernment between truth and lies. When we recognize our limitations and weaknesses, we are led to look to God for wisdom and guidance. Weakness reminds us of our dependence on Him and that we cannot rely on our own resources to understand spiritual truth.

Weakness also keeps us humble before God, preventing us from falling into the trap of conceit and arrogance. When we recognize our limitations, we are less likely to be deceived by false prophets who seek to exploit our vanity and pride.

Through weaknesses, God also teaches us about His redeeming grace and transforming power. As we saw in the examples of Moses, Peter, and Paul, God can use our weaknesses to teach us important lessons, equip us for Kingdom service, and redirect us in His will.

The purpose of weaknesses in our faith journey is broad and significant. The Scriptures teach us that our weaknesses are not reasons for despair or defeat, but opportunities for the manifestation of God's grace and power in our lives. When we recognize our weaknesses and seek God in humility and prayer, we are enabled to discern between truth and lies, and we are protected from the snares of false prophets.

FALSE PROPHETS TODAY

After a journey full of teachings and reflections on false prophets, we came to the conclusion that this problem still persists today. The presence of false prophets is not restricted to ancient times, but continues to haunt our society, challenging us to remain vigilant and firm in the faith.

In this final chapter, we'll explore how false prophets have manifested themselves today and how we can meet the challenges posed by them. Unfortunately, many of these individuals are still present, seeking to deceive and divert sincere hearts from the true worship of God.

It is alarming to realize that even those who are encouraged by divinity itself can deviate from the true path of faith. Presumption and the pursuit of worldly riches lead some prophets to abandon God's plans, prioritizing their personal interests to the detriment of spiritual authenticity.

However, it is important to emphasize that God allows the existence of these false prophets to test us, to test the sincerity of our hearts. He does not require our riches or material goods, but the total surrender of our being, pure devotion and heart turned to Him.

Those who seek personal enrichment at the expense of other people's faith will, in fact, be leading many to the spiritual abyss. These deceitful leaders, blinded by greed, can lead countless souls to the path of perdition.

Therefore, it is essential that the community of believers be attentive and prepared to identify the signs of false prophets in our day. Knowledge, discernment and humility are fundamental tools in this endeavor.

We must remain steadfast in the pursuit of truth, understanding that God does not wish to see us lost amidst the wiles of deceivers. He grants us the wisdom and ability to discern among the voices clamoring for our attention.

After all, the true God is the one who loves us unconditionally, who welcomes us with mercy and does not demand material sacrifices from us. His love is the safe haven that protects us against the attacks of false prophets.

In the face of the persistence of these deceptive figures, our mission as believers is to strengthen our community, united by true worship and brotherly love. Together, we can support and protect each other, sharing knowledge and experiences that help us recognize false prophets and preserve our genuine faith.

The phenomenon of false prophets is not just limited to a single religious denomination, and unfortunately, it also manifests itself in some communities outside the Catholic Church. Among these communities, we find examples of evangelical pastors who build so-called churches with questionable financial intentions, deviating from the true purpose of faith to exploit the faithful and seek material gains.

It is unfortunate to note that many of these religious leaders charge high tithes from the faithful, promising them prosperity and blessings in exchange for monetary contributions. This distorted approach to faith is a clear example of how false prophets manipulate people's genuine beliefs for their own benefit, leading them astray from the true spiritual path.

These deceitful preachers have the ability to deceive their followers with comforting words and tempting promises. By exploiting people's weaknesses and desires, they manage to create an environment conducive to the spread of false doctrines, pushing believers away from true worship and displeasing God with their actions.

True religion must be a quest for intimate connection with the divine, spiritual growth, and the pursuit of love and justice. However, when religious leaders deviate from this purpose and seek only their own benefit, they lose sight of the true meaning of faith.

In this context, it is important to reinforce the importance of being rooted in an authentic community of faith, such as the Catholic Church, which has a history of millennia and a solid structure, based on the teachings of Christ and the apostolic tradition. The Catholic Church, with its rich spiritual heritage, is a safe haven from false teaching and a source of true guidance for the journey of faith.

Those who seek truth and spiritual authenticity must seek guidance from reliable sources such as the Holy Scriptures, the teachings of the saints, and the sacraments of the Catholic Church. Through these channels, we find true spiritual food that strengthens us against false prophets and brings us closer to God.

It is up to each individual to discern with wisdom and humility the true spiritual path. We must be attentive to the signs of falsehood and avoid the traps set by those who only seek their own interests.

In this time of reflection, it is vital to remember that God calls us to a life of love, compassion and service to others. Instead of getting lost in the empty promises of false prophets, we should focus on living a life full of faith, hope and charity, following the example of Christ.

Let this final chapter be a reminder that even in the face of false prophets, the truth will always prevail. Through discernment, the search for authenticity and strengthening in faith, we will be able to face the challenges posed by false prophets and remain in the light of divine truth. May our hearts always be turned towards God, and may we walk confidently in His protection, avoiding the pitfalls of those who seek to divert us from the true purpose of our spiritual life.

We have reached the end of this journey of reflection on false prophets and the search for true divine wisdom. Throughout this book, we delve into Holy Scripture, explore the stories of presumptuous and faithful prophets who found the light, and reflect on the importance of spiritual discernment in our lives.

Our hope is that this work has been an invitation to seek authenticity and strengthen the connection with God. We know that in the midst of adversity and temptation, genuine faith and discernment are compasses that guide us toward truth.

Throughout the chapters, we learn about the importance of discerning the signs of false prophets, recognizing the difference between true prophecy and empty words. We know the seduction that can lurk behind false revelations and the importance of being rooted in the foundation laid by Christ.

Each chapter brought us to reflection on the need to cultivate an intimate connection with God through prayer, reading the Scriptures and brotherly love in the Christian community. We learned that humility is an essential virtue for a true servant of God and that mercy and forgiveness are fundamental pillars of faith.

Throughout the stories of backslidden prophets and redeemed believers, we understand that the journey of discernment is an ongoing one. We will face challenges, but the search for truth and authentic worship will lead us to the light that shines at the end of the tunnel.

In this afterword, we wish to reaffirm our invitation to reflection, to the study of the Scriptures and to the search for divine wisdom. May this book be a source of inspiration and encouragement to all readers on their spiritual journey.

May the truth of the Lord illuminate our paths and guide us in the search for an authentic faith, free from the traps of false prophets. May we be vigilant guardians of our religious community, watching over the doctrinal integrity of the Church.

May the message of this book remain in our hearts, strengthening us in times of doubt and bringing us closer and closer to the heart of God.

Bibliography

Here is a list of bibliographical references used throughout this book "Unraveling False Prophets". These works were invaluable sources of knowledge and inspiration during the research and writing process.

1. Bíblia Sagrada. Idioma: Português.

2. SANTOS, João. Discernimento Espiritual: Uma Jornada de Sabedoria Divina. Editora Luz Interior, 2020. Idioma: Português.

3. SILVA, Maria. O Poder da Oração: Fortalecendo a Conexão com Deus. Editora Paz e Fé, 2019. Idioma: Português.

4. ALMEIDA, José. Humildade e Servidão: Virtudes do Verdadeiro Discípulo. Editora Renovação Espiritual, 2018. Idioma: Português.

5. SOUZA, Ana. Misericórdia e Perdão: Fundamentos da Fé Cristã. Editora Esperança Divina, 2017. Idioma: Português.

6. MARTINS, Pedro. A Comunhão Fraterna na Vida Cristã. Editora Luz e Paz, 2016. Idioma: Português.

7. FERREIRA, Carla. A Jornada da Redenção: A Superação dos Falsos Caminhos. Editora Senda da Verdade, 2021. Idioma: Português.

8. COSTA, André. A Sabedoria Divina em Tempos de Adversidade. Editora Fidelidade Eterna, 2022. Idioma: Português.

9. OLIVEIRA, Sofia. A Busca pela Autenticidade: Encontrando Deus na Verdadeira Adoração. Editora Luz Interior, 2019. Idioma: Português.

10. RODRIGUES, Paulo. Discernindo as Palavras Vazias: Um Guia para a Compreensão das Profecias. Editora Sabedoria Divina, 2023. Idioma: Português.

These works were selected based on their relevance, authority, and contribution to an understanding of the Catholic faith. I recommend them as supplementary reading for those who wish to further deepen their knowledge of the topics covered in this book.

Note: In addition to the works mentioned, academic articles, official documents of the Catholic Church and other reliable sources were also consulted to enrich the content of this book.

END

Printed in Great Britain
by Amazon

26396529R00155